Charles Martel
&
the Battle of Tours

Charles Martel

Charles Martel
&
the Battle of Tours

The Defeat of the Arab Invasion of Western Europe
by the Franks, 732 A.D

ILLUSTRATED

Edward Creasy
G. L. Strauss
Charles King
and
Walter Copland Perry

LEONAUR

Charles Martel & the Battle of Tours
The Defeat of the Arab Invasion of Western Europe by the Franks, 732 A.D
Edward Creasy
G. L. Strauss
Charles King
and
Walter Copland Perry

ILLUSTRATED

FIRST EDITION

Leonaur is an imprint of Oakpast Ltd
Copyright in this form © 2018 Oakpast Ltd

ISBN: 978-1-78282-746-7 (hardcover)
ISBN: 978-1-78282-747-4 (softcover)

http://www.leonaur.com

Publisher's Notes

Contents

The Battle of Tours, A.D. 732
By Edward Creasy

The broad tract of Champaign country which, intervenes between the cities of Poitiers and Tours is principally composed of a succession of rich pasture lands, which are traversed and fertilized by the Cher, the Creuse, the Vienne, the Claine, the Indre, and other tributaries of the River Loire. Here and there, the ground swells into picturesque eminences; and occasionally a belt of forest land, a brown heath, or a clustering series of vineyards, breaks the monotony of the widespread meadows; but the general character of the land is that of a grassy plain, and it seems naturally adapted for the evolutions of numerous armies, especially of those vast bodies of cavalry which principally decided the fate of nations during the centuries that followed the downfall of Rome, and preceded the consolidation of the modern European powers.

This region has been signalised by more than one memorable conflict; but it is principally interesting to the historian, by having been the scene of the great victory won by Charles Martel over the Saracens, *A.D.* 732, which gave a decisive check to the career of Arab conquest in Western Europe, rescued Christendom from Islam, preserved the relics of ancient and the germs of modern civilization.

Sismondi and Michelet have underrated the enduring interest of this great appeal of battle between the champions of the Crescent and the Cross. But, if French writers have slighted the exploits of their national hero, the Saracenic trophies of Charles

CHARLES MARTEL IN THE BATTLE OF POITIERS.

Martel have had full justice done to them by English and German historians. Gibbon devotes several pages of his great work, to the narrative of the Battle of Tours, and to the consideration of the consequences which probably would have resulted, if Abderrahman's enterprise had not been crushed by the Frankish chief.

★★★★★★

In vol. 7, Gibbon's remark, that if the Saracen conquest had not then been checked, "Perhaps the interpretation of the *Koran* would now be taught in the schools of Oxford, and her pulpits might demonstrate to a circumcised people the sanctity and truth of the revelation of Mahomet," has almost an air of regret.

★★★★★★

Schlegel, (*Philosophy of History*), speaks of this "mighty victory" in terms of fervent gratitude; and tells how "the arms of Charles Martel saved and delivered the Christian nations of the West from the deadly grasp of all-destroying Islam;" and Ranke, (*History of the Reformation in Germany*, vol. i.), points out, as "one of the most important epochs in the history of the world, the commencement of the eighth century; when, on the one side, Mahommedanism threatened to overspread Italy and Gaul, and on the other, the ancient idolatry of Saxony and Friesland once more forced its way across the Rhine. In this peril of Christian institutions, a youthful prince of Germanic race, Karl Martell, arose as their champion; maintained them with all the energy which the necessity for self-defence calls forth, and finally extended them into new regions."

Arnold ranks the victory of Charles Martel even higher than the victory of Arminius, (History of the later Roman Commonwealth, vol. ii.), "among those signal deliverances which have affected for centuries the happiness of mankind." In fact, the more we test its importance, the higher we shall be led to estimate it; and, though the authentic details which we possess of its circumstances and its heroes are but meagre, we can trace enough of its general character to make us watch with deep interest this encounter between the rival conquerors of the decaying Roman empire. That old classic world, the history of which occupies so large a portion of our early studies, lay, in the eighth century of our era, utterly exanimate and overthrown. On the north the German, on the south the Arab, was rending away its provinces.

At last the spoilers encountered one another, each striving for the full mastery of the prey.

Although three centuries had passed away since the Germanic conquerors of Rome had crossed the Rhine, never to repass that frontier stream, no settled system of institutions or government, no amalgamation of the various races into one people, no uniformity of language or habits, had been established in the country, at the time when Charles Martel was called on to repel the menacing tide of Saracenic invasion from the south.

Gaul was not yet France. In that, as in other provinces of the Roman empire of the West, the dominion of the Caesars had been shattered as early as the fifth century, and barbaric kingdoms and principalities had promptly arisen on the ruins of the Roman power. But few of these had any permanency; and none of them consolidated the rest, or any considerable number of the rest, into one coherent and organized civil and political society.

The great bulk of the population still consisted of the conquered provincials, that is to say, of Romanised Celts, of a Gallic race which had long been under the dominion of the Caesars, and had acquired, together with the slight infusion of Roman blood, the language, the literature, the laws, and the civilization of Latium.

Among these, and dominant over them, roved or dwelt the German victors: some retaining nearly all the rude independence of their primitive national character; others, softened and disciplined by the aspect and contact of the manners and institutions of civilized life. It is to be borne in mind, that the Roman empire in the West was not crushed by any sudden avalanche of barbaric invasion. The German conquerors came across the Rhine, not in enormous hosts, but in bands of a few thousand warriors at a time.

The conquest of a province was the result of an infinite series of partial local invasions, carried on by little armies of this description. The victorious warriors either retired with their booty, or fixed themselves in the invaded district, taking care to keep sufficiently concentrated for military purposes, and ever ready for some fresh foray, either against a rival Teutonic band, or some hitherto unassailed city of the provincials. Gradually, however, the conquerors acquired a desire for permanent landed possessions. They lost some of the restless thirst for novelty and adventure which had first made them throng beneath the banner of the boldest captains of their tribe, and leave their native forests for a roving military life on the left bank of the Rhine. They were converted to the Christian faith; and gave up with their old creed much of the ferocity, which must have been fostered in the spirits of the ancient warriors of the North by a mythology which promised, as the reward of the brave on earth, an eternal cycle of fighting and drunkenness in heaven.

But, although their conversion and other civilizing influences operated powerfully upon the Germans in Gaul; and although the Franks (who were originally a confederation of the Teutonic tribes that dwelt between the Rhine, the Maine, and the Weser) established a decided superiority over the other conquerors of the province, as well as over the conquered provincials, the country long remained a chaos of uncombined and shifting elements.

The early princes of the Merovingian dynasty were generally occupied in wars against other princes of their house, occasioned by the frequent subdivisions of the Frank monarchy: and the ablest and best of them had found all their energies tasked to the utmost to defend the barrier of the Rhine against the Pagan Germans, who strove to pass that river and gather their share of the spoils of the empire.

The conquests which the Saracens effected over the southern and eastern provinces of Rome were far more rapid than those achieved by the Germans in the north; and the new organisations of society which the Moslems introduced were summarily and uniformly enforced.

Exactly a century passed between the death of Mohammed

The Battle of Poitiers

and the date of the Battle of Tours. During that century the followers of the Prophet had torn away half the Roman empire; and, besides their conquests over Persia, the Saracens had overrun Syria, Egypt, Africa, and Spain, in an unchequered and apparently irresistible career of victory.

Nor, at the commencement of the eighth century, was the Mohammedan world divided against itself, as it subsequently became. All these vast regions obeyed the Caliph; throughout them all, from the Pyrenees to the Oxus, the name of Mohammed was invoked in prayer, and the *Koran* revered as the book of the law.

It was under one of their ablest and most renowned commanders, with a veteran army, and with every apparent advantage of time, place, and circumstance, that the Arabs made their great effort at the conquest of Europe north of the Pyrenees. The victorious Moslem soldiery in Spain, including Syrians, Moors, Saracens, Greek renegades, Persians, and Copts, and Tartars was eager for the plunder of more Christian cities and shrines, and full of fanatic confidence in the invincibility of their arms.

The Moslems had overthrown the Visigoth power in Spain and their eager expectations of new wars were excited to the utmost on the re-appointment by the Caliph of Abderrahman Ibn Abdillah Alghafeki to the government of that country, *A.D.* 729, which restored them a general who had signalised his skill and prowess during the conquests of Africa and Spain, whose ready valour and generosity had made him the idol of the troops, who had already been engaged in several expeditions into Gaul, so as to be well acquainted with the national character and tactics of the Franks; and who was known to thirst for revenge for the slaughter of some detachments which had been cut off on the north of the Pyrenees.

In addition to his cardinal military virtues, Abderrahman is described by the Arab writers as a model of integrity and justice. The first two years of his second administration in Spain were occupied in severe reforms of the abuses which under his predecessors had crept into the system of government, and in extensive preparations for his intended conquest of Gaul. Besides the

THE ISLAMIC EMPIRE

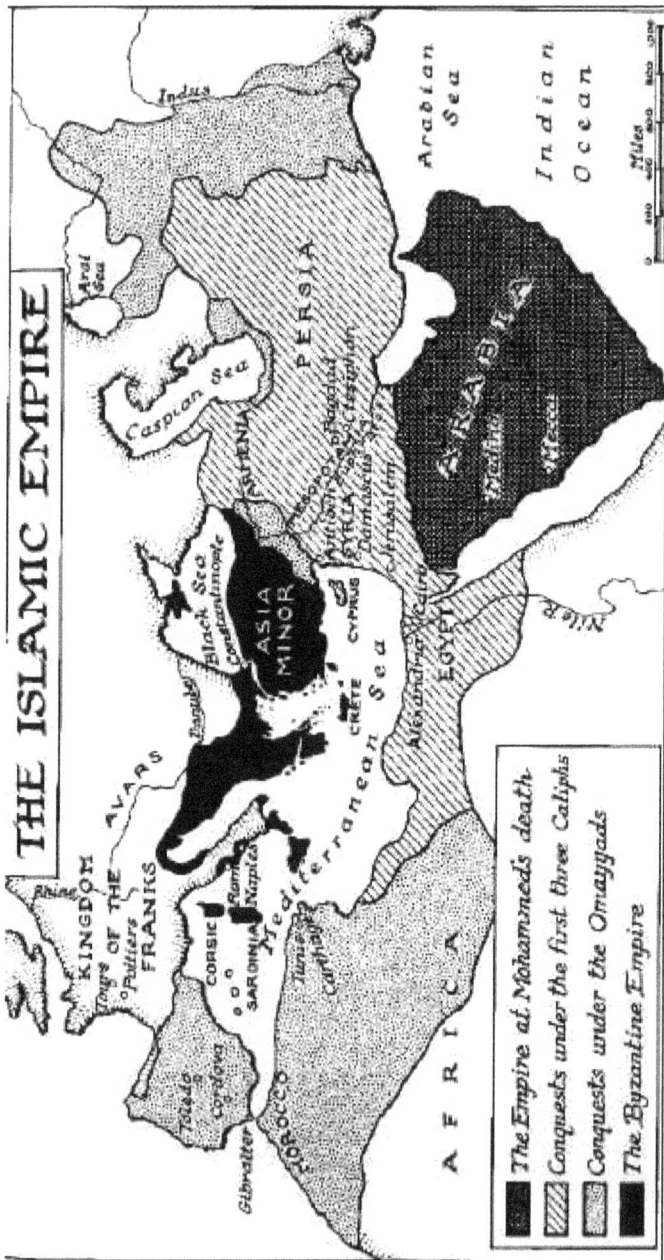

Indus

Aral Sea

Caspian Sea

PERSIA

Arabian Sea

Indian Ocean

Miles

ARABIA

ARMENIA

Medina

Mecca

Rhine

KINGDOM

AVARS

Danube

Black Sea

Constantinople

Bagdad

Ctesiphon

SYRIA

Damascus

Jerusalem

Antioch

Tours OF THE
Poitiers FRANKS

ASIA MINOR

CYPRUS

CRETE

Mediterranean Sea

Alexandria

EGYPT

Niger

Toledo
Cordova

CORSICA

SARDINIA

Rome
Naples

MOROCCO

Gibraltar

Tunis
Carthage

AFRICA

The Empire at Mohammed's death.

Conquests under the first three Caliphs

Conquests under the Omayyads

The Byzantine Empire

troops which he collected from his province, he obtained from Africa a large body of chosen Berber cavalry, officered by Arabs of proved skill and valour: and in the summer of 732 he crossed the Pyrenees at the head of an army which some Arab writers rate at eighty thousand strong, while some of the Christian chroniclers swell its numbers to many hundreds of thousands more.

Probably the Arab account diminishes the actual number, but of the two keeps nearer to the truth. It was from this formidable host, after Eudes, the Count of Acquitaine, had vainly striven to check it, after many strong cities had fallen before it, and half the land been overrun, that Gaul and Christendom were at last rescued by the strong arm of Prince Charles, who acquired a surname, (Martel—*The Hammer*), like that of the war-god of his forefathers' creed, from the might with which he broke and shattered his enemies in the battle.

The Merovingian kings had sunk into absolute insignificance, and had become mere puppets of royalty before the eighth century. Charles Martel, like his father, Pepin Heristal, was Duke of the Austrasian Franks, the bravest and most thoroughly Germanic part of the nation: and exercised, in the name of the titular king, what little paramount authority the turbulent minor rulers of districts and towns could be persuaded or compelled to acknowledge. Engaged with his national competitors in perpetual conflicts for power, engaged also in more serious struggles for safety against the fierce tribes of the unconverted Frisians, Bavarians, Saxons, and Thuringians, who at that epoch assailed with peculiar ferocity the Christianised Germans on the left bank of the Rhine, Charles Martel added experienced skill to his natural courage, and he had also formed a militia of veterans among the Franks.

Hallam has thrown out a doubt whether, in our admiration of his victory at Tours, we do not judge a little too much by the event, and whether there was not rashness in his risking the fate of France on the result of a general battle with the invaders. But, when we remember that Charles had no standing army, and the independent spirit of the Frank warriors who followed his standard, it seems most probable that it was not in his power to adopt the cautious policy of watching the invaders, and wearing out their strength by delay. So dreadful and so wide-spread were the ravages of the Saracenic light cavalry throughout Gaul, that it must have been impossible to restrain for any length of time the indignant ardour of the Franks.

If Charles could have persuaded his men to look tamely on while the Arabs stormed more towns and desolated more districts, he could not have kept an army together when the usual period of a military expedition had expired. If, indeed, the Arab account of the disorganisation of the Moslem forces be correct, the battle was as well-timed on the part of Charles as it was, beyond all question, well-fought.

The monkish chroniclers, from whom we are obliged to glean a narrative of this memorable campaign, bear full evidence to the terror which the Saracen invasion inspired, and to the agony of that great struggle. The Saracens, say they, and their king, who was called Abdirames, came out of Spain, with all their wives, and their children, and their substance, in such great multitudes that no man could reckon or estimate them. They brought with them all their armour, and whatever they had, as if they were thenceforth always to dwell in France.

Then Abderrahman, seeing the land filled with the multitude of his army, pierces through the mountains, tramples over rough and level ground, plunders far into the country of the Franks, and smites all with the sword, insomuch that when Eudo came to battle with him at the River Garonne, and fled before him, God alone knows the number of the slain. Then Abderrahman pursued after Count Eudo, and while he strives to spoil and burn the holy shrine at Tours, he encounters the chief of the Austrasian Franks, Charles, a man of war from his youth, to whom Eudo had sent warning. There for nearly seven days they strive intensely, and at last they set themselves in battle array; and the nations of the north standing firm as a wall, and impenetrable as a zone of ice, utterly slay the Arabs with the edge of the sword. (*Script. Gest. Franc.*)

The European writers all concur in speaking of the fall of Abderrahman as one of the principal causes of the defeat of the Arabs; who, according to one writer, after finding that their leader was slain, dispersed in the night, to the agreeable surprise of the Christians, who expected the next morning to see them issue from their tents, and renew the combat. One monkish chronicler puts the loss of the Arabs at 375,000 men, while he says that only 1,007 Christians fell—a disparity of loss which he feels bound to account for by a special interposition of Providence. I have translated above some of the most spirited passages of these writers; but it is impossible to collect from them anything like a full or authentic description of the great battle itself or of the operations which preceded or followed it.

Though, however, we may have cause to regret the meagreness and doubtful character of these narratives, we have the great advantage of being able to compare the accounts given of Abderrahman's expedition by the national writers of each side. This is a benefit which the inquirer into antiquity so seldom can obtain, that the fact of possessing it, in the instance of the Battle of Tours, makes us think the historical testimony respecting that great event more certain and satisfactory than is the case in many other instances, where we possess abundant details respecting military exploits, but where those details come to us from the annalist of one nation only; and where we have, consequently, no safeguard against the exaggerations, the distortions, and the fictions which national vanity has so often put forth in the garb and under the title of history. The Arabian writers who recorded the conquests and wars of their countrymen in Spain, have narrated also the expedition into Gaul of their great *emir*, and his defeat and death near Tours in battle with the host of the Franks under King Caldus, the name into which they metamorphose Charles.

★★★★★★

The Arabian chronicles were compiled and translated into Spanish by Don Jose Antonio Conde, in his *Historia de la Dominacion de los Arabos en España*, published at Madrid in 1820. Conde's plan, which I have endeavoured to follow,

17

Moslem cavalryman

was to preserve both the style and spirit of his oriental authorities, so that we find in his pages a genuine Saracenic narrative of the wars in Western Europe between the Mohammedans and the Christians.

★★★★★★

They tell us how there was war between the count of the Frankish frontier, (Eudo), and the Moslems, and how the count gathered together all his people, and fought for a time with doubtful success. The Arabian chroniclers say:

But, Abderrahman drove them back; and the men of Abderrahman were puffed up in spirit by their repeated successes, and they were full of trust in the valour and the practice in war of their *emir*. So, the Moslems smote their enemies, and passed the river Garonne, and laid waste the country, and took captives without number. And that army went through all places like a desolating storm. Prosperity made those warriors insatiable. At the passage of the river, Abderrahman overthrew the count, and the count retired into his stronghold, but the Moslems fought against it, and entered it by force, and slew the count; for everything gave way to their scimitars, which were the robbers of lives.

All the nations of the Franks trembled at that terrible army, and they betook them to their King Caldus, (Charles), and told him of the havoc made by the Moslem horsemen, and how they rode at their will through all the land of Narbonne, Toulouse, and Bordeaux, and they told the king of the death of their count.

Then the king bade them be of good cheer, and offered to aid them. And in the 114th year, (of the *Hegira*), he mounted his horse, and he took with him a host that could not be numbered, and went against the Moslems. And he came upon them at the great city of Tours. And Abderrahman and other prudent cavaliers saw the disorder of the Moslem troops, who were loaded with spoil; but they did not venture to displease the soldiers by ordering them to abandon everything except their arms and warhorses.

And Abderrahman trusted in the valour of his soldiers,

and in the good fortune which had ever attended him. But (the Arab writer remarks) such defect of discipline always is fatal to armies. So Abderrahman and his host attacked Tours to gain still more spoil, and they fought against it so fiercely that they stormed the city almost before the eyes of the army that came to save it; and the fury and the cruelty of the Moslems towards the inhabitants of the city were like the fury and cruelty of raging tigers. It was manifest that God's chastisement was sure to follow such excesses; and fortune thereupon turned her back upon the Moslems.

Near the River Owar, (probably the Loire), the two great hosts of the two languages and the two creeds were set in array against each other. The hearts of Abderrahman, his captains, and his men were filled with wrath and pride, and they were the first to begin the fight. The Moslem horsemen dashed fierce and frequent forward against the battalions of the Franks, who resisted manfully, and many fell dead on either side, until the going down of the sun. Night parted the two armies: but in the grey of the morning the Moslems returned to the battle. Their cavaliers had soon hewn their way into the centre of the Christian host. But many of the Moslems were fearful for the safety of the spoil which they had stored in their tents, and a false cry arose in their ranks that some of the enemy were plundering the camp; whereupon several squadrons of the Moslem horsemen rode off to protect their tents.

But it seemed as if they fled; and all the host was troubled. And while Abderrahman strove to check their tumult, and to lead them back to battle, the warriors of the Franks came around him, and he was pierced through with many spears, so that he died. Then all the host fled before the enemy, and many died in the flight. This deadly defeat of the Moslems, and the loss of the great leader and good cavalier Abderrahman, took place in the hundred and fifteenth year.

It would be difficult to expect from an adversary a more

explicit confession of having been thoroughly vanquished, than the Araba here accord to the Europeans. The points on which their narrative differs from those of the Christians,—as to how many days the conflict lasted, whether the assailed city was actually rescued or not, and the like,—are of little moment, compared with the admitted great fact that there was a decisive trial of strength between Frank and Saracen, in which the former conquered.

The enduring importance of the Battle of Tours in the eyes of the Moslems, is a attested not only by the expressions of "the deadly battle," and "the disgraceful overthrow," which their writers constantly employ when referring to it, but also by the fact that no further serious attempts at conquest beyond the Pyrenees were made by the Saracens.

Charles Martel, and his son and grandson, were left at leisure to consolidate and extend their power. The new Christian Roman Empire of the West, which the genius of Charlemagne founded, and throughout which his iron will imposed peace on the old anarchy of creeds and races, did not indeed retain its integrity after its great ruler's death. Fresh troubles came over Europe; but Christendom, though disunited, was safe. The progress of civilization, and the development of the nationalities and governments of modern Europe, from that time forth, went forward in not uninterrupted, but, ultimately, certain career.

SYNOPSIS OF EVENTS BETWEEN THE BATTLE OF TOURS, A.D. 732, AND THE BATTLE OF HASTINGS, 1066.

A.D. 768—814. Reign of Charlemagne. This monarch has justly been termed the principal regenerator of Western Europe, after the destruction of the Roman empire. The early death of his brother, Carloman, left him sole master of the dominions of the Franks, which, by a succession of victorious wars, he enlarged into the new Empire of the West. He conquered the Lombards, and re-established the Pope at Rome, who, in return, acknowledged Charles as *suzerain* of Italy. And in the year 800, Leo III., in the name of the Roman people, solemnly crowned Charlemagne at Rome, as Emperor of the Roman Empire of the West. In Spain, Charlemagne ruled the country between the Pyrenees and the Ebro; but his most important conquests were effected on the eastern side of his original kingdom, over the Sclavonians of Bohemia, the Avars of Pannonia, and over the previously uncivilized German tribes who had remained in their fatherland.

The old Saxons were his most obstinate antagonists, and his wars with them lasted for thirty years. Under him the greater part of Germany was compulsorily civilized, and converted from Paganism to Christianity. His empire extended eastward as far as the Elbe, the Saal, the Bohemian mountains, and a line drawn from thence crossing the Danube above Vienna, and prolonged to the Gulf of Istria. (Hallam's *Middle Ages*.)

Throughout this vast assemblage of provinces, Charlemagne established an organised and firm government. But it is not as a mere conqueror that he demands admiration.

In a life restlessly active, we see him reforming the coinage, and establishing the legal divisions of money, gathering about him the learned of every country; founding schools and collecting libraries; interfering, with the air of a king, in religious controversies; attempting, for the sake of commerce, the magnificent enterprise of uniting the Rhine and the Danube, and meditating to mould the discordant code of Roman and barbarian laws into an uniform system. (Hallam.)

814—888. Repeated partitions of the empire and civil wars between Charlemagne's descendants. Ultimately, the kingdom of France is finally separated from Germany and Italy. In 962, Otho the Great, of Germany, revives the imperial dignity.

827. Egbert, king of Wessex, acquires the supremacy over the Anglo-Saxon kingdoms.

832. The first Danish squadron attacks part of the English coast. The Danes, or Northmen, had begun their ravages in France a few years earlier. For two centuries Scandinavia sends out fleet after fleet of sea-rovers, who desolate all the western

kingdoms of Europe, and in many cases effect permanent conquests.

871—900. Reign of Alfred in England. After a long and varied struggle, he rescues England from the Danish invaders.

911. The French king cedes Neustria to Hrolf the Northman. Hrolf (or Duke Rollo, as he thenceforth was termed) and his army of Scandinavian warriors, become the ruling class of the population of the province, which is called after them Normandy.

1016. Four knights from Normandy, who had been on a pilgrimage to the Holy Land, while returning through Italy, head the people of Salerno in repelling an attack of a band of Saracen *corsairs*. In the next year many adventurers from Normandy settle in Italy, where they conquer Apulia (1040), and afterwards (1060) Sicily.

1017. Canute, King of Denmark, becomes King of England. On the death of the last of his sons, in 1041, the Saxon line is restored, and Edward the Confessor (who had been bred in the court of the Duke of Normandy), is called by the English to the throne of this island, as the representative of the House of Cerdic.

1035. Duke Robert of Normandy dies on his return from a pilgrimage to the Holy Land, and his son William (afterwards the conqueror of England) succeeds to the dukedom of Normandy.

MOSLEM WARRIOR

Moslem and Frank; or, Charles Martel and the rescue of Europe

By G. L. Strauss

PART 1. THE MOSLEMS

From the perspective of the invasion of Europe we should look at the year as pivotal. After decades of internal strife Abd-el-Malek became *Khalif* in 685 *A.D.* and quickly consolidated his position. The Greeks had instead of boldly drawing the sword to wrest Asia Minor, Palestine, and Syria from the enfeebled grasp of the divided Saracens, they were content with obtaining from Abd-el-Malek a considerable increase of the tribute.

Abd-el-Malek, relieved thus from his apprehensions of a war with the Eastern empire, could now turn his undivided attention to the impending struggle with the rival *Khalif* of Mecca. After five years' fierce and doubtful contest, Abdallah was at length defeated in a decisive battle, and compelled to take refuge in Mecca; here he defended himself for seven months against Abd-el-Malek' s vastly superior forces. At last, in a general assault, the valiant son of Zobeir was slain; his fall decided that of the city, and the Saracen empire was thus again united under one ruler (692). As soon as Abd-el-Malek saw himself sole and undisputed Khalif, he threw off the badge of servitude to the Eastern empire, which the internal dissensions and troubles of the preceding years had compelled him to submit to. He discontinued the payment of the stipulated tribute, and even wrested another province, Armenia, from the feeble hands of the Byzantine Caesars.

Hassan, the governor of Egypt, was charged with the task to reconquer the north of Africa. That brave and skilful commander, after having subdued the provinces of the interior, carried his victorious arms to the sea-coast, and took, by a sudden assault, the fortifications of Carthage, the metropolis of Africa, (697). However, the unexpected arrival of a powerful Greek fleet, with a numerous and well-appointed army, (it would appear, from Leo Africanus, that a considerable body of Goths formed part of the army of relief), on board, compelled the Arabian general to evacuate his recent conquest, and to retire to Cairoan. But Abd-el-Malek had resolved to annex North Africa to his dominions at any cost; he prepared therefore during the winter a powerful armament by sea and land, and in spring, 698, Hassan appeared once more before Carthage, and compelled the *praefect* and patrician John, who commanded the Greek forces, to evacuate the city.

Soon after, he defeated him again in the neighbourhood of Utica, and a precipitate embarkation alone saved the remains of the Byzantine Army from absolute annihilation. Carthage was reduced to a heap of ruins. But Hassan had soon to encounter a more formidable enemy: a prophetess arose among the Moors, or Berbers, of the interior, and boldly challenged the Arabian invaders to make good their claim to the land which they had fondly deemed subdued with the expulsion of the Greeks. Cahina was the name of this extraordinary woman, who seemed to have discovered the secret of breathing into her people a spirit of enthusiasm superior even to the fanaticism of the Moslems. In a single day Africa was lost again to the Saracens, and the humbled Hassan retired to the confines of Egypt, where he expected, five years, the promised succour of the *Khalif.*

But Queen Cahina's order to destroy the cities, and to cut down the fruit-trees, filled the Christian population of the coast with apprehension and anger; and when Hassan at last made his reappearance in the province, he was hailed, even by the most zealous Catholics, as a deliverer and saviour. The royal prophetess boldly accepted battle; but she was slain, and her army was put to the rout (705). Still the spirit of resistance survived, and

Hassan's successor, the aged but fiery Musa Ben Nassir, had to quell a new insurrection of the Moorish tribes. He and his two sons, Abdallah and Abdelaziz, succeeded so well, however, that not only did the Berbers submit to the Khalif, but they even embraced the religion of Islam, and became henceforth as one people with their Arabian conquerors.

Abd-el-Malek was the first *Khalif* to establish a national mint, both for silver and gold coin (695); the gold coins were imitations of the Roman gold *denar*, with an inscription proclaiming the unity of the God of Mohammed; the Arabs called these gold coins, *dinars*; their value was about eight shillings sterling, (in 1854). It would appear they struck also double, and half, *dinars*. The silver coin might represent a value of fivepence or sixpence English money. Abd-el-Malek died in 705. He was succeeded by his son Walid, a prince who, indeed, did not inherit the activity, vigour, and decision of his father; but was on the other hand, free also from the cruelty and the low avarice that stained the character of Abd-el-Malek.

Walid loved and encouraged arts and sciences, and more especially architecture: he built the splendid mosque of the Ommiades at Damascus, at an expense of half a million sterling; he rebuilt also Mohammed's mosque at Medina, on a larger and more magnificent scale. He had the good fortune to be served by clever ministers and great generals, whose energy, valour, and enterprise amply made up for the personal indolence and inactivity of the *Khalif*, and imparted a glory to his reign, rivalling that of Omar's. One of his lieutenants, Catibah (the camel driver), added to the Saracen empire the spacious regions between the Oxus, the Jaxartes, and the Caspian Sea, with the rich and populous commercial cities Carizme, Bochara, and Samarcand (707—710).

From Samarcand, the victorious general sent his master a daughter of Phirouz, or Firuz, the son of the unfortunate Yezdegerd, the last of the Sassanide rulers of Persia, who became Walid's wife. Mohammed, one of Catibah's colleagues, displayed the banner of Islam on the opposite banks of the Indus (712); and in the same year, Fargana, the residence of the Chagan of the Turks, was taken by Catibah, who advanced as far as Cashgar, where he received an embassy from the Emperor of China. Walid's brother, Moslemah, one of the most redoubtable of the Mussulman warriors known to history, defeated the Chazars in the Caucasus, and annexed Galatia and other parts of Asia Minor to the empire of his brother (710).

But the greatest and most glorious conquest was that of Spain. As early as the time of Othman, the Arabs had cast a longing eye upon the fair land of Handalusia, and their piratical squadrons had more than once ravaged the Spanish coast.

★★★★★★

Handalusia signifies, in Arabic, the country of the West; and the Arabs applied the name not only to the modern province of Andalusia, but to the whole peninsula of Spain. The attempted derivation of the name of Andalusia from the Vandals (Vandalusia) is most improbable. Lembke travels still farther out of the way of all rational probability, by assigning the etymological paternity of the name to Andalos, whom the Arabians number among Noah's grandchildren.

★★★★★★

The Gothic king, Wamba, had defeated one of their expeditionary corps in 675. Since that time no further attempt had been made on the kingdom of the Visigoths; but the latter, beholding with apprehension the establishment of the Arabian power in North Africa, had, in 697, aided the Byzantine emperor in the attempted relief of Carthage. The king of Spain possessed on the African coast the fortress of Ceuta (*Septa* or *Septum*), one of the columns of Hercules, which is divided by a narrow strait from the opposite pillar or point on the European coast. This fortress was held at the beginning of the eighth century by the Gothic Count Julian, brother-in-law of Oppas, archbishop of Toledo and Seville, whose brother, Witiza, was then King of Spain.

In 709, Musa made an attempt to reduce Ceuta, and subdue the small portion of Mauritania which was still wanting to the conquest of North Africa; but he was repulsed by Count Julian with considerable loss, and would most probably have relinquished his project upon Spain, had not internal dissensions among the Gothic magnates unexpectedly opened to him a fair prospect of success. King Witiza had attempted to reform the truly appalling licentiousness of the Spanish clergy, and to curb the overgrown power of the nobility; but lacking both the crafty wile of the eleventh Louis of France, and the strong despotic will of the Tudors of England, his well-meant efforts simply led to his own deposition (710), which he survived only a few months.

The clergy and nobility elected a king after their own heart, in the person of Roderic, a grandson of King Reccaswinth (or Receswinth, 649-672). The two sons of Witiza, and their uncle Oppas, conspired to overthrow the new monarch, who, it would appear, had been indiscreet enough to express his intention of removing Count Julian from his Andalusian and Mauritanian commands, the moment he should think himself sufficiently powerful to give due force to his royal decrees.

✶✶✶✶✶✶

This would certainly seem to have been the true cause of Julian's defection; the story of the seduction or viola-tion of his daughter Florinda (surnamed *la Cava, i.e.*, the wicked), lacks all true historic foundation. Mariana, the Jesuit historian, to whom we are chiefly indebted for this pretty tale, was too apt to draw on his lively imagination, where historical evidence failed him.

✶✶✶✶✶✶

The threatened count was readily induced to join the party of the conspirators; but dreading lest the force which they could bring into the field, should prove unavailing against the mon-arch's power, he, who had hitherto been the staunchest defender of his country, did not hesitate to betray her to the Saracen foe, and to open wide the portals that had been entrusted to his honour and patriotism to guard. He and his fellow-conspira-tors endeavoured to soothe the misgivings of conscience with Musa's deceptive assurance, that he did not intend to establish himself in Spain, but would rest content with a share of the spoil.

As soon as Musa had obtained Walid's sanction to the con-templated enterprise, he sent off an expedition of only four ves-

Brigandine warrior

sels, with five hundred men on board, to explore the coast of the coveted land. Tarif Abu Zara, the commander of this force, landed on the opposite side of the strait, and marched eighteen miles into the interior, to the castle and town of the traitor Count of Ceuta, (July 710). (The place on which the Arabs landed is marked to the present day by the name of their chief Tarif—Tarifa—; on the coast they bestowed the name of the Green Island—Algesiras or Algezire.) His glowing report of the wealth of the country, decided Musa to send over a more powerful expedition under the command of his freedman, Tarik Ben Zayad.

The miserable Julian supplied the means of transport. Five thousand Arabs and seven thousand Moors landed at the European pillar of Hercules, Mount Calpe, which became, henceforth, the Mountain of Tarik—*Gebel al Tarik*, a name corrupted afterwards into the present appellation of Gibraltar (April, 711). Here Tarik formed a strongly entrenched camp, and gathered around him the friends of Julian, and also many Jews who were fired with the most deadly hatred against their Christian persecutors, that had, for more than a century, oppressed and hunted down this doomed people with a malignity such as religious fervour alone can excite and sustain. Counts Edeco and Theodemir, who had been commanded by the king to expel the intruders, were defeated with great slaughter; and a seasonable reinforcement from Africa swelled Tarik's ranks to above 30,000 men.

Roderic, conscious at last of the magnitude of the danger that threatened to overwhelm his throne and his people, gathered the flower of the Gothic nation around him, and marched at the head of 100,000 men to encounter the foreign invaders. In the neighbourhood of Cadiz, at Xeres de la Frontera, on the Guadelete, the hostile armies met. Three days were spent in desultory, though bloody fighting; on the fourth day, the actual battle commenced.

When night spread her sable wings, and bade the slaughter cease for a while, more than half of the Saracen forces lay stretched dead on the ground they had come to conquer; and had not the vile defection of the most reverend father in God, the Archbishop of Toledo, and his two nephews, to whom Roderic's generous or foolish (it may be read both ways) confidence had entrusted the most important post, broken the ranks of the Christians, the severed head of Musa's freedman might have graced the battlements of Toledo. As it was, it took three days to scatter the remains of the Gothic army; and many a Saracen, and many a Christian traitor to his country, had to bite the dust before Tarik could pen his laconic "Praise be to *Allah!*—we have conquered." (July 19-26, 711). The hapless king of the Goths was either slain in the fight or drowned in the waters of the Guadalquivir.

The field of Xeres decided the fate of the Gothic monarchy; nearly the whole of Spain submitted to Tarik with such extraordinary rapidity, that the good old Musa, envious of his freedman's success and fame, bade him arrest his victorious course, until he himself should arrive to gather the last and fairest fruits of the victory. Tarik, however, added Cordova and Toledo, the capital of the Gothic kingdom, to the list of his conquests, and advanced as far as the Bay of Biscay, where the failure of land at last compelled him to stop.

Here, he received an angry and imperious summons from his jealous chief; who had, meanwhile, himself crossed over from Africa, at the head of ten thousand Arabs and eight thousand Moors, and had taken Seville, and was besieging Merida. The latter city, though valiantly defended, was at last compelled to surrender. Midway between Merida and Toledo, Tarik met his chief, who received him with cold and stately formality, and demanded a strict account of the treasures of the conquered kingdom. The unfortunate lieutenant speedily found that Musa would not readily forgive his presumption of subduing Spain in the absence of his general: he saw himself ignominiously deprived of his command, and thrown into prison; and Musa carried his resentment so far, that he ordered the conqueror of Spain to be publicly scourged.

Walid's imperative commands compelled Musa to restore Tarik to his position; and the valiant man, who had been so ungenerously and unworthily treated by the jealous old chief, assisted him with his accustomed zeal, in achieving the conquest of the still unsubdued parts of the peninsula. At the end of 712, all resistance had ceased on the part of the Christians, with the exception of the valiant prince Theodemir, who defended himself several months longer in Orihuela, and obtained, at last, most favourable terms from Musa's son, Abdelaziz, (5th April, 713); and the invincible Pelagius, or Pelayo, and Petrus, who, in the Asturian, Gallician, and Biscayan Tallies, laid the foundation of a new Christian empire in Spain; destined, after a time, to renew the struggle and ultimately to expel the foreign invaders.

Musa was a very old man—but though the colouring of his beard, and other little expedients of art, might fail to obliterate the physical ravages wrought by eighty-eight years of life, and by the fatigues and privations of fifty campaigns—yet the vigour of his mind, and the youthful ardour that fired his breast, remained unimpaired: and, like that marvellous old man of a later period, great Dandalo, the approach of ninety found him revolving enterprises of stupendous magnitude; aye, no less than the conquest of Gaul, Italy, Germany, and the Greek empire. He was preparing to pass the Pyrenees, and bid the kingdom of the Franks cease to exist, when an imperious command from Damascus, called both him and Tarik thither, to render an account of their proceedings to the commander of the faithful.

★★★★★★

Musa had fought in Syria; he had assisted Moawiyah in the reduction of Cyprus (648), and had held the government of that island; he had subsequently been governor of Irak, and after this, governor of Egypt; Sardinia, Majorca, and Minorca, also had felt his presence.

Some historians lead Musa (in 712) into the Narbonnese Gaul, there are strong reasons to reject this as an erroneous supposition; it is more than doubtful whether the old chief ever passed the Pyrenees.

★★★★★★

Tarik obeyed; Musa delayed complying with the *Khalif's* summons, until a second and still more peremptory message left

33

the old chief no other alternative but obedience or open rebellion: and, as his own loyalty, or that of his troops, put the latter out of question, he set at once diligently about preparing for his return to Damascus. He confided the government of Spain to his son, Abdelaziz; that of Africa, to his son, Abdallah. Taking with him immense treasures in gold and silver, and, among others, the famous emerald table of Solomon, encircled with pearls and gems—a spoil of the Romans from the east, and which, it would appear, had fallen into the hands of Alaric, in the sack of Rome, (410, *A.D.*); and attended by thirty Gothic princes, 400 nobles, and 18,000 male and female captives of humbler degree, he set out from Ceuta on his way to Damascus.

★★★★★★

The statement made by some historians, that Ætius presented this table as a gift to Torismund, after the victory of Chalons (451), seems to rest on a very slender foundation; and so, I am inclined to think, do the 365 feet of gems and massive gold so liberally bestowed upon the table by Oriental writers. Another tradition substitutes, as the gift of the Roman patrician, the famous Missorium, or great golden dish for the service of the communion table, which is stated to have weighed 500 pounds, and to have been adorned with a profusion of gems.

★★★★★★

At Tiberias, in Palestine, he received a private message from Suleiman, or Soliman, the brother and presumptive heir of Walid, informing him that the *Khalif* was dying, and commanding him, as he valued Soliman's friendship, to reserve his triumphal entry into Damascus for the inauguration of the new reign.

Musa, who might deem Soliman's anger less dangerous than the resentment of the *Khalif* should he recover, disregarded the injunction, and pursued his march to Damascus, where he arrived just in time to afford the dying Walid the gratification of beholding the spoils of Africa, and of Spain, soon after which, the most powerful of the *Khalifs* bowed his head to the stroke of the mighty master of kings and emperors (October, 714).

★★★★★★

Some historians make Musa arrive *after* the death of Walid; and some place the latter event a year later (716). The records of the period of the early *Khalifs* are so confused and contradictory that it is by no means easy always to ascertain the correct date of an event; the difficulty is considerably increased by the error into which some historians have fallen, of confounding the lunar year of the Mohammedans with the solar year of the Julian era. The common lunar year of the *Hegira* has 354 days; but the Mohammedans count, in a cyclus of 30 years, 11 leap years of 355 days (the 2nd, 5th, 7th, 10th, 13th, l6th, 18th, 2lst, 24th, 26th and 29th years of the cyclus.

★★★★★★

His successor, Soliman, was an able and energetic prince, but of a despotic and ruthless disposition. Musa was arraigned at the judgment seat of the new *Khalif*, for abuse of power and disobedience to orders. The unworthy treatment which the victor of Xeres had suffered at the hands of his jealous chief, was avenged by a similar indignity inflicted upon the latter: the veteran commander was publicly scourged, and then kept waiting A whole day before the palace gate, till the "mercy" of Soliman accorded him a sentence of exile to Mecca. He was, moreover, adjudged to pay to the public treasury, a fine of 200,000 pieces of gold.

Afraid lest the sons of the despoiled and insulted old man, should attempt to avenge the injuries of their father, the worthy son of Abd-el-Malek secretly dispatched to Africa and Spain, decrees commanding the extermination of Musa's family; and, by a refinement of cruelty worthy of a Caligula, Caracalla, or Justinian II. he had the head of Abdelaziz presented to the bereaved father, with an insulting question, whether he knew the features of the rebel? "I know his features," exclaimed the hapless old man, in a paroxysm of grief and indignation; "he was loyal and true. May the same fate overtake the base authors of his death!" — — —Musa's death, a few weeks after, of the anguish of a broken heart, spared Soliman an additional crime.

The victor of Xeres fared but little better than his ancient commander; though, indeed, he was not made to expiate by

Moslem warrior

death, imprisonment, or exile, the great services which he had rendered his country. Catibah, who had every reason to dread a similar fate as Musa's and Tarik's, rose in arms against the jealous tyrant of Damascus, and had the good fortune to meet with a glorious death on the battlefield.

Soliman resolved to render his reign famous by the overthrow of the Greek empire, and the conquest of Constantinople. His preparations, both by land and sea, were made on a gigantic scale. His brother, the redoubtable Moslemah, invaded Asia Minor at the head of 70,000 foot and 50,000 horse, with an immense train of camels, (716). The city of Tyana fell into the hands of the Moslems, and Amorium was closely besieged by them. The troops in Amorium were commanded at the time by General Leo, a native of Isauria. The original name of this remarkable man, was Konon; his father had come over from Asia Minor to Thrace, and had settled as a grazier there. He must have acquired considerable wealth in that lucrative business, since he could afford a gift of 500 sheep to the Imperial camp, to procure for his son admission into the guards of Justinian.

The personal strength of the young soldier, and his dexterity in all martial exercises attracted the notice of the emperor, who speedily advanced him to the higher grades of military rank. Anastasius II. confided to him the command of the Anatolian *legions*, and it was in this capacity that he defended Amorium against the Saracens. One of those sudden revolutions so frequent in the Byzantine court, compelled Anastasius to hand over the sceptre to an obscure officer of the revenue, who assumed the name of Theodosius III.

General Leo refused to acknowledge the new emperor, and managed so skilfully, that not only did the troops under his command invest him with the imperial purple, but the Arabs, it would appear, accorded him and his army free and undisturbed departure from Amorium. He marched upon Constantinople, and Theodosius seeing himself in danger of being abandoned by the very troops who had so recently exalted him, willingly resigned to the hands of the general and emperor of the Oriental troops, the sceptre which, moreover, he had accepted with extreme reluctance only. He was permitted to retire with his son to the shelter of a monastery, where he had ample time to paint golden letters, an occupation which marvellously suited the natural indolence of his disposition.

Leo, third of the name, who figures in history usually as the Isaurian, or the Iconoclast, was fully aware of the intention of the Arabs to attempt the reduction of Constantinople; he, therefore, made every preparation which military experience could suggest, or engineering skill devise, to give them a fitting reception. In July, 717, after the reduction of Pergamus, Moslemah transported his army from Asia to Europe, across the Hellespont or Dardanelles, at the most narrow part of the passage (from Abydos to Sestos); and thence, wheeling his troops round Gallipoli, Heraclea, and the other Thracian cities of the Propontis, or Sea of Marmara, he invested Constantinople on the land side.

An offer made by the Greeks, to purchase the withdrawal of the besieging forces by the payment of a piece of gold for each inhabitant of the city, was contemptuously rejected; and Moslemah pushed on the operations of the siege with the greatest vigour, but without any corresponding success, the Isaurian repelling every attack with a bravery and determination, such as the Saracens had but little expected to see displayed by the apparently effete Greeks. Moslemah's hopes were swelled high, however, by the arrival of the navies of Syria and Egypt, to the number of 1800 vessels, (of small size, of course), with 60,000 men on board. The Saracen commander fixed a night for a general assault by land and sea, and proudly boasted that by the morning the city should be his.

When that morning came, the Greek fire had done its work; and scarce a vestige remained of the proud fleet, or of those who had manned it; and ten thousand Arabs and Persians slain, bore witness how fiercely Moslemah had assaulted the defences of Byzantium, and how bravely and vigorously the Isaurian and his gallant troops had repulsed the hostile multitudes. From this check, Moslemah essayed in vain to recover: he became soon painfully conscious that the conviction of invincibility, which had hitherto so materially contributed to the great successes of the Saracen arms, was, if not altogether destroyed, at least considerably shaken. His assaults were now repulsed with apparent ease almost, and all his attempts at surprises were defeated by the ever watchful Isaurian.

One hope still remained to restore the ancient supremacy of the Moslem arms: Khalif Soliman had gathered a formidable host of Arabians, Persians, and Turks, and was preparing to lead them to his brother's assistance. The eyes of both the besiegers and the besieged were anxiously turned towards the Khalif's camp near Chalcis (or Kinnisrin) in Syria; and Leo was endeavouring, by gifts and promises, to attract an army of Bulgarians from the Danube to pit them against the Saracens; and thus, perchance, to free the Byzantine empire from all danger, by the mutual destruction of its Barbarian foes. But it so happened that the Commander of the Faithful could not command his appetite; a meal of two scores or so of eggs, and a matter of six or seven pounds of figs, followed up by a dessert of marrow and sugar, proved too much for even his well-seasoned stomach; he paid with his life the penalty of his gluttony (717). He had appointed his cousin, Omak Ben Abdelaziz, to succeed him in the *khalifate*.

Omar, second of the name, was a most estimable man, but a very indifferent prince; much fitter, indeed, to be the head of a monastery of ascetics, than of a powerful empire. The first act of his reign was to order the cessation of the Syrian armaments, which might have been a wise measure, had it been accompanied by the recall of Moslemah and his forces from the siege of Constantinople. His neglect of the latter measure entailed upon the unfortunate natives of the sultry climes of Egypt and Arabia, the unspeakable hardships of a most severe winter, passed in a frozen camp. In spring (718), he made an effort to relieve their wants, and to fill up the gaps which cold, famine, and disease had made in the ranks of the besieging army.

Two numerous fleets were sent on this errand, one from Alexandria, the other from the ports of Africa. They succeeded, indeed, in landing the stores and reinforcements, but they found it as vain to contend against the Greek fire, as the armada which, the year before, had so proudly threatened to erase the Roman name from among the nations. Meanwhile, the Bulgarians had been bribed into an alliance with the Greek emperor, and these savage auxiliaries proved formidable antagonists to the exhausted and half-starved Asiatics. Still the intrepid Moslemah was not dismayed, and although he was compelled to relinquish all further attempts upon the defences of the city, he defeated, on his part, all attacks made on his camp: until, at length, Khalif Omar sent him the welcome order to raise the siege, (August, 718).

The retreat of the Arabian forces was effected without delay or molestation; but of the fleet, tempests destroyed what the fire of Callinicus had spared, and of 700 vessels that had proudly sailed forth, five only returned to the port of Alexandria, to tell the sad tale of the disastrous loss of their companions. Byzantium was saved, and the victorious Isaurian found himself at liberty to prepare for his meditated warfare against canvas, wood, brass, and marble.

The good and pious Omar distinguished his reign chiefly by the abolition or "repeal" of the curse against Ali and his adherents which had for nearly sixty years been daily pronounced from the pulpits (719). By this act of simple justice, and by his somewhat hasty and incautious attempts to reform the fearful abuses which had crept into the administration of the empire under his predecessors, he excited the determined hostility of his own family, and of the *vizirs* and high officers of state. A dose of poison removed him (720). His successor, Yezid II., had none of his virtues, but most of the vices of his other predecessors of the line of Ommiyah.

It was in the reign of this prince, and in that of his successor, that the family Hashem, in two of its branches, *viz.* the Alides, or Fatimites, *i. e.* the descendants of Ali and Fatima, and the Abassides, that is the descendants of Abbas, the uncle of the prophet, began to urge their claims to the throne of the *Khalifs*. Indeed, Mohammed, the great grandson of Abbas, was secretly acknowledged as the true commander of the Faithful, by a considerable body of the inhabitants of Chorasan, and his son Ibrahim was even enabled to hoist the black flag of the Abassides in that province; the gloomy banner was triumphantly borne onward by Abu Moslem, the intrepid and invincible champion of the Abassides, the King-maker of the East, but, who was fated at last, like the English King-maker, to experience the usual gratitude of princes.

★★★★★★

In the separation of parties, the green colour was adopted by the Alides, or Fatimites, the black colour by the Abassides, and the white colour by the Ommiades; these colours were displayed respectively by the several parties, not only in their standards but also in their garments and turbans.

★★★★★★

From the Indus to the Euphrates, the East was convulsed by the fearful struggle between the white and the black factions, and the fairest provinces of Asia were deluged with blood to void the ancient quarrel between Ommiyah and Hashem, and to decide which of two equally vile races of despots had the better right to trample on God's fair creation. The struggle terminated for a time in 750, with the overthrow and almost total extirpation of the Ommiades—but of this hereafter.

Yezid died in 722 or 723, of grief for the death of a favourite concubine. He was succeeded by his brother Hesham, a prince not altogether destitute of good qualities. Hesham had to contend against the Fatimite Zeid, the grandson of Hassan, who was, however, speedily overcome, and had to pay with his life the penalty of his ambition. The struggle against the more successful Abassides has been mentioned in the preceding paragraph.

After Musa's departure from Spain, and the murder of his son Abdelaziz, Ajub was proclaimed by the Arabian and Moorish troops, governor of the Spanish peninsula; he fixed his residence at Cordova. Under him and his more immediate successors numerous colonies came over to Spain from various parts of the Saracen dominions in Asia and Africa; of these the royal legion of Damascus was planted at Cordova; that of Emesa at Seville; that of Chalcis at Jaen; that of Palestine at Algezire and Medina Sidonia. The Egyptian bands were permitted to share with the original conquerors their establishments of Murcia and Lisbon.

The immigrants from Yemen and Persia were located round Toledo, and in the inland country; and ten thousand horsemen of Syria and Irak, the children of the purest and most noble Arabian tribes, settled in the fertile seats of Grenada. (Gibbon.)

Ajub's successor in the government of Spain, El Horr Ben Abderrahman resolved to annex to the dominions under his sway the Gallic province of Septimania or Languedoc, of which the eastern part, with Narbonne and Carcassone, was still remaining in the hands of the Visigoths; the western part, Aquitaine and Thoulouse having been severed from the Gothic kingdom in 508, by Clovis. But he was defeated and driven back by the Christians; in consequence of the ill-success of his operations, the *Khalif* removed him from the command, and named El Zama governor in his stead.

That bold and skilful general speedily succeeded in reducing the whole of the Narbonnese province (720); whence he marched into Aquitaine, and laid siege to Thoulouse. Here he found a more formidable foe to encounter—the Franks, who were ultimately to check the further advance of Islam and its followers into the fairest provinces of Europe. The history of that nation, and of its successful leader against the Saracen invaders, forms the subject of the second part of this volume.

PART 2: THE FRANKS

THE FRANK CONFEDERACY.—CLOVIS, THE FOUNDER OF THE FRANK MONARCHY

A great deal of labour and ingenuity has been wasted in futile endeavours to trace the origin of a *distinct* Frank nation; however, after exhausting every possible means of research, and every probable and improbable suggestion of fancy, the most rational writers are now agreed in looking upon the supposed existence of a distinct Frank nation as a myth, and in believing that the name of Franks or Freemen was assumed, most probably about the middle of the third century after Christ, by a league of several Germanic nations, of whom the most important were the Sigambrians and the Catti.

★★★★★★

42

Still we must not omit to state that the lays of ancient Germany, and the old Chronicles of the country, exhibit singular agreement in the reproduction of the popular tradition which makes the nation of the Franks come from Troy. However, after all, this makes no great difference, as even the most strenuous believers in the existence of a distinct nation of Franks, fully admit that as early as the third century (the time when the name of the Franks first appears in history) that name included *several* Germanic nations. By some the Thuringians are given as a *branch* of the Frank nation.

★★★★★★

The former constituted, with the Bructeri, the Chamavians, the Chattuarii, and perhaps also part of the Batavians, the lower branch of the confederacy; towards the end of the third century their settlements extended along the eastern bank of the Rhine, from the Lippe down to the mouth of the great German river; they occupied also the island of the Batavians, and the land between the Rhine and Meuse, and down to the Scheld. From the settlement of the Sigambrians on the Yssel or Sala, this branch of the confederacy received the name of the *Salian* Franks.

★★★★★★

Some, however, derive the name from the Old German word *saljan*, *i. e.* to grant, in reference to part of the territory occupied by the Salian Franks having been *granted* to them by the Romans (by Carausius, in 287, confirmed at a later period by Julian the Apostate) Leo derives the name from the Celtic word, *Sal*, *i e.* the sea.

★★★★★★

The Catti, the Ambsivarians, and some other tribes, (including perhaps even the Hermunduri, or Thuringians?) constituted the upper branch of the confederacy.

The upper Franks extended their settlements from the lands between the Mein and Lippe gradually along both banks of the Rhine, from Mayence to Cologne; and, although repeatedly driven back by the Romans, they ultimately retained possession of the left bank of the river; whence they were also called

Riparian or Ripuarian Franks (from the Latin *ripa*, bank, shore).

The Franks repeatedly invaded Gaul, more particularly in the reigns of Valerian, (253—260), and of Gallienus (260—268); and though the Romans boast of numerous victories achieved at the time against them, under the leadership of Posthumus, the general of Valerian, but who afterwards usurped the empire in Gaul.

★★★★★★

Valerian was taken prisoner by Sapor, King of Persia, in 260, who is said to have treated the fallen emperor with the greatest indignity. Valerian died in captivity.

Posthumus was one of the nineteen usurpers who rose against Gallienus in the several provinces of the empire. The writers of the Augustan history have magnified the number to thirty.

★★★★★★

Yet it is certain that the Franks not only carried their devastations from the Rhine to the foot of the Pyrenees, but numbers of them actually crossed these mountains, and ravaged Spain during twelve years; when they had exhausted that unfortunate country, they seized on some vessels in the ports of Spain, and crossed over to the coast of Africa, where their sudden appearance created the utmost consternation.

The Emperor Probus defeated the Franks in 277, and transported a colony of them to the sea-coast of Pontus, where he established them with a view of strengthening the frontier' against the inroads of the Alani. But impelled by their unconquerable love of country and freedom, they seized on a number of vessels in one of the harbours of the Euxine, sailed boldly through the Bosphorus and the Hellespont, and, cruising along the coast of the Mediterranean, made frequent descents upon the coasts of Asia, Greece, and Africa, and actually took and sacked the opulent city of Syracuse, in the island of Sicily; whence they proceeded to the Columns of Hercules, where they made their way into the Atlantic, and coasting round Spain and Gaul, reached the British Channel, sailed through it, and landed ultimately in safety, and richly laden with spoil, on the Batavian shore.

In 287, the Menapian Carausiuss, who usurped the imperial

purple in Britain, granted to the Franks the island of the Batavians, and the land between Meuse and Scheld. Constantius (293), and Constantine (313), expelled them from these provinces; the Ripuarians also felt the heavy hand of Constantine, and of his son Crispus; the latter expelled them for a time from the left bank of the Rhine. But Julian found both the Salians and the Ripuarians in their old places; and, though successful against both (357 and 858), contented himself with the partial expulsion of the Ripuarians and the Chamavians, leaving the Sigambrians in quiet possession of the island of the Batavians, and the extensive district of Brabant, which they had occupied, on condition that they should henceforth hold themselves subjects and auxiliaries of the Roman empire. However, the expelled tribes soon made their reappearance on the banks of the Rhine, and, at the end of the fourth century, the Franks had regained complete possession of their old quarters.

Stilicho, the great minister and general of the contemptible Honorius, made it one of the first acts of his administration to secure the alliance of the warlike Franks against the enemies of Rome (395). He succeeded so well, it would appear, that the Franks actually handed over to the discretion of his justice, one of their kings or dukes, Marcomir, who was accused of having violated the faith of treaties; the accused prince was exiled to Tuscany, his brother Sunno, who attempted to avenge the insult which he deemed had been put upon the nation by this degradation of the dignity of one of its chiefs, met with a harsher fate at the hands of his own countrymen: he was slain by them; and the princes whom Stilicho had appointed, were cheerfully acknowledged.

★★★★★★

History names Pharamond as the first King of the Franks; the author of the *Gesta Francorum* makes that prince the son of Marcomir, the king mentioned in the text; and there appears to be little doubt indeed, but that the Franks had established the right of hereditary succession somewhat before the time of Clodion, the reputed son of Pharamond.

The fact that Stilicho himself was of German (Vandalian) extraction, may account in some degree for this extraordinary subserviency of the Franks to the will and wishes of the master of the "Western Empire. On this occasion, the Franks had engaged to protect the province of Gaul against invasion from the side of Germany. An opportunity of proving their sincerity and fidelity to Rome, or perhaps rather to the great minister who had made the treaty of alliance with them, offered in the year 406, when the confederated nations of the Vandals, the Alani, the Suevi, and the Burgundians, were moving in a body to the Rhine with the intention of invading Gaul; and most honestly and valiantly indeed did the Franks acquit themselves of the duty undertaken by them.

It so happened that the Vandals were the first to make their appearance on the bank of the river; proudly relying on their numbers they attempted to force the passage, without awaiting the coming up of the other confederated nations. They paid the penalty of their rashness; twenty thousand of them were slain, among them their king, Godigisolus; and the opportune arrival of the Alani, whose squadrons trampled down the infantry of the Franks, alone saved the nation of the Vandals from total destruction. Attacked by the combined forces of the confederates, the Franks were at last compelled to give way. On the 31st December, 406, the Suevi, the Alani, the Vandals, and the Burgundians, crossed the frozen Rhine without further opposition, and thus entered the defenceless provinces of Gaul, where the Burgundians formed a lasting settlement, the other nations of the confederacy proceeding subsequently further on to Spain and Lusitania.

History leaves us in the dark as to the period when the Franks first submitted to the sway of *hereditary* princes; but this much seems certain, that it must have been long before the time of Pharamond; and also that their longhaired kings, did not derive the name of Merovingians, from Meroveus, the grandson of Pharamond, but either from some more ancient Meroveus; or perhaps from Merve, the name which the Meuse receives after its union with the Waal (an arm of the Rhine); or from the same name of a castle near Dortrecht, supposed to have been the family seat of the Frankian kings.

★★★★★★

The fashion of long hair was among the Franks for a time, the somewhat exclusive privilege of the royal family; the members of which wore their locks hanging down in flowing ringlets on their back and shoulders; while the rest of the nation were obliged to shave the hind part of the head, and to comb the hair over the forehead.

★★★★★★

It would appear that Pharamond, the son of Marcomir, was elevated on the buckler, about 410, and that his son Clodion succeeded him in 428. (Elevation on a buckler was the ceremony by which the Franks invested their chosen leader with military command.) It is somewhat doubtful whether these two kings held sway over the Ripuarians as well as over the Salians, or even over all the nations which constituted the league of the latter. Clodion had his residence at Dispargum, in Brabant, somewhere between Louvain and Brussels. (Duisborch? According to some historians and geographers, Duisburg, on the right bank of the Rhine.)

Soon after his accession, this prince invaded Belgic Gaul, took Tournay and Cambray, and advanced as far as the river Somme. He was surprised and defeated in the plains of Artois, by Ætius, the general of the Western empire (430); but that astute politician deemed it the wiser course to secure the friendship of the powerful leader of the warlike Franks, and therefore conceded to him free possession of the conquered province. Clodion died about 448 (450?) He left two sons who disputed his succession. All we can gather from the very confused and contradictory accounts of this period, is that the younger of the two sons, whose name is not mentioned, was raised on the buckler by the Ripuarian, the elder, Mervey or Meroveus, by the Salian Franks; and that the former joined Attila in his invasion of Gaul, and fought on the side of the Huns in the great Battle of Chalons (451); whilst Meroveus, with his Salians joined the standard of

47

Ætius, and combated on the side of the Romans and Visigoths.

★★★★★★

Most historians make Meroveus, the younger of the two sons of Clodion; and, after his father's death, they send him to Rome to implore the protection of Ætius. Now, it is next to impossible that the *beardless youth*, whom Priscus states to have seen at Rome (about 449 or 450), could have been Meroveus, since the son of that prince, Childeric, was within ten years after exiled by the Franks on account of his excesses and his despotic sway. The young man whom Priscus saw was most probably Childeric, who may have been sent to Rome by his father, Meroveus, to renew the alliance which Clodion had made with Ætius.

★★★★★★

Mervey's son, Childeric, offended the Franks by his excesses and his arbitrary proceedings: he was deposed by them, and was compelled to seek a refuge at the court of the King of the Thuringians, Bisinus or Basinus. The Franks having thus disposed of their king, proceeded to bestow the royal dignity Upon Ægidius, the Roman master-general of Gaul, who, after the compelled abdication and the most suspicious death of the Emperor Majorian, in 461, had refused to acknowledge the successor forced upon the acceptance of the Roman Senate by the all-powerful Patrician Ricimer, the instigator of Majorian's fall, and had assumed the sovereignty over the remnant of the Gallic province which still obeyed the Roman sway.

However, a few years after, the Franks, who found the Roman system of taxation more oppressive and objectionable than any act of Childeric's, recalled that prince, and, under his guidance, expelled the "tax-gatherers" (465). Ægidius acquiesced with a good grace in a change which he had not the power to oppose. Childeric had been most hospitably entertained by King Bisinus; but the hospitality extended to him by the wife of that monarch, Queen Basina, was, by all accounts, still more liberal than that shown to the interesting guest by her worthy husband.

After Childeric's restoration, Basina left her husband, and rejoined her lover: the fruit of this voluntary union was Clovis, who, at the age of fifteen, succeeded, by his father's death, to the rule of that portion of the Salian territory, over which Childeric had held sway, and which was confined to the island of the Batavians, with the ancient dioceses of Tournay and Arras; for the custom of the Franks to divide the treasures and territories of a deceased duke or king equally among his sons, had had the natural effect to split the kingdom of Pharamond into several parts independent of each other.

Clovis combined with an insatiable ambition, all the qualities requisite to satisfy that all-absorbing passion. His personal bravery was controlled and directed by cool and consummate prudence. He wielded the *francisca* (the battle-axe of the Franks) with formidable strength and skill; and he did not hesitate, when occasion required, to make his own soldiers feel the weight of his arm and the precision of his aim. He subjected the barbarians whom he commanded to the strict rules of a severe discipline which he enforced with unbending rigor. A crafty and astute politician, he was endowed with the most essential requisites for success, patience and perseverance.

In the pursuit and accomplishment of his ambitious designs, he trampled on every law of God and nature; no feeling of pity ever stayed, no fear of retribution ever restrained, his murderous hands. He was indeed the worthy progenitor of a line of princes fit to take the proudest place among the highest aristocracy of crime, to put to the blush the Neros, the Caligulas, the Domitians, the Caracallas, the Elagabalus of imperial Rome, and to rank with the Bourbons, the Hapsburgs and the Tudors. At the age of twenty, he made war upon Syagrius, the son of Ægidius, who had inherited from his father the city and diocese of Soissons, and whose sway was acknowledged also by the cities and territories of Rheims, Troyes, Beauvais and Amiens.

In alliance with his cousin Ragnachar, King of the Franks of Cambray, and some other Merovingian princes, he defeated Syagrius at Soissons, and reduced in the brief space of a few months the remnant of the Roman dominion in Gaul, and which had survived ten years the extinction of the Western empire (486). Syagrius fled to Thoulouse, where he flattered himself to find a safe asylum; but in vain: Alario II., the son of the great Euric, was a minor, and the men who governed the kingdom of the Visigoths in his name, were but too readily intimidated by the threats of Clovis, and pusillanimously delivered up the hapless fugitive to certain death. A few years after (491), Clovis enlarged his dominions towards the east by the ample diocese of Tongres. In 493, he married the Burgundian princess Clotilda, who, in the midst of an Arian court, had been educated in the Nicean faith.

★★★★★★

The kingdom of the Burgundians, which had been established in 407, was divided, in 470, among the four sons of King Gonderic; Hilperic, or Chilperic, the father of Clotilda, fixed his residence at Geneva; Gundobald at Lyons; Godegesil at Besançon, and Godemar at Vienne (in Dauphiné).

A war broke out between the brothers, in which Gundobald conquered and took prisoner Hilperic and Godemar; the latter committed suicide; the former was put to death by his inhuman brother Gundobald, and his wife and his two sons shared his fate; his two daughters were spared, and one of them, Clotilda, was brought up at the court of Lyons; and, as chance would have it, in the Catholic faith, though Gundobald himself, like most of the Christian princes of the time, professed the Arian doctrine. Gundobald would gladly have refused Clovis the hand of his niece, had he dared to brave the anger of the powerful Frankish chief.

Clotilda, on her part, was overjoyed at the prospect of an alliance with a king, whose ambition might be turned to good account for the pursuit of her own vengeful projects against the murderer of her father; with a pagan, whose conversion to the Nicean creed would gain her beloved Catholic church a formidable champion against the hated Arian heretics. Gundobald had scarcely parted with his niece, and her father's treasures, when the pious princess displayed her Christian spirit, by ordering her Frankish escort to burn down the Burgundian villages through which they were passing, and when she saw the flames rising, and heard the despairing cries of the unfortunates who were thus being deprived of their homes, she lifted up her voice, and praised the God of Athanasius—the *holy* Chlotildis!

★★★★★★

Clotilda's endeavours to convert her husband to Christianity were not very successful at first, though he consented to the baptism of his first-born son; the sudden death of the infant, which the ignorant and superstitious Pagan was inclined to attribute to the anger of his gods, had well-nigh proved fatal to any further attempt at conversion; still the beauty and blandishments of the pious queen succeeded at last in overcoming the scruples and apprehensions of her husband, and gaining his consent to a repetition of the experiment: this time the infant survived, and Clovis began to listen with greater favour to the exhortations of his Christian spouse.

In the year 496, the Alemanni, who occupied both banks of the Rhine, from the source of that river to its conflux with the Mein and the Moselle, and had spread themselves over the modern provinces of Alsace and Lorraine, invaded the territories of Sigebert, the King of the Ripuarian Franks, who had his seat at Cologne.

★★★★★★

The Alemanni were also, like the Franks, a league of several Germanic nations, among whom the Tencteri, the Usipetes, and most probably a portion of the Suevi, were the most important. The favourite etymology of the name, Allemanni or All-Men, as meant to denote at once the various lineage, and the common bravery of the component members of the league, is a little fanciful perhaps, yet not more so, or rather not quite so much so, as some other etymologies of the name indulged in by the learned.

★★★★★★

Sigebert, unable to resist the invaders single-handed, invoked the powerful aid of his cousin, Clovis, and the latter hastened at once to the rescue. He encountered the invaders in the plain of Tolbiac (Zülpich), about twenty-four miles from Cologne. A fierce battle ensued. For several hours it raged with unabated fury, without any decided advantage being gained by either party; at length the Franks gave way, and the Alemanni raised shouts of victory. Clovis saw his dream of power and ambition rapidly fading away; in his extremity he invoked the God of Clotilda and the Christians, to grant him the victory over his enemies, which service he vowed duly to acknowledge, by consenting to be baptised. (The invocation as given by Gregory of Tours, is rather naïve, a pretty plain hint: no victory, no belief, no baptism.)

Resolved, however, to do his share also towards the achievement of the victory which he was imploring the Christian Lord of Hosts to vouchsafe him, he rallied his discomfited troops, and placing himself at their head, led them on again to the attack, and by his valour and conduct, succeeded in restoring the battle. The franciscas, and the heavy swords of the Franks, made fearful havoc in the hostile ranks; the king, and many of the most valiant chiefs of the Alemanni, were slain, and ere evening the power of one of the fiercest and most warlike nations of Germany, was annihilated. Pursued by the victorious Franks into the heart of their forests, the Alemanni were forced to submit to the yoke of the conqueror; some of their tribes fled to the territory of the Gothic king of Italy, Theodoric, who assigned them settlements in Rhaetia, and interceded, with his brother-in-law, in favour of the conquered nation. (Theodoric had lately married Albofleda (Audofleda or Andefleda), the sister of Clovis.)

In his distress, Clovis had vowed to adore the God of the Christians, if He would succour him; the danger past, and the victory achieved, the perfidious Frank would gladly have made light of his vow, but for the incessant importunities of Clotilda, and of Remigius, the Catholic bishop of Rheims. On the day of Christmas in the same year, (496), Clovis was baptised in the Cathedral of Rheims with 3000 of his warlike subjects; and the remainder of the Salians speedily followed the example. As the kings of the Goths, Burgundians, and Vandals were Arians, and even the Greek emperor, Anastasius, was not quite free from the taint of heresy; the Bishop of Rome, Anastasius II., overjoyed at the conversion of the powerful king of the Franks to the Nicean faith, hailed the neophyte as the "Most Christian King."

The conversion of Clovis to the Catholic faith stood him in excellent need in his schemes of further aggrandisement. His arms were henceforward supported by the favour and zeal of the Catholic clergy, more especially in the discontented cities of Gaul, under the sway of the Arian kings of the Visigoths and the Burgundians. The Armoricans, or Bretons, in the north-western provinces of Gaul, who had hitherto bravely and successfully resisted all attempts of the Fagan chief to conquer them, were now gradually induced to submit to an equal and honourable union with a Christian people, governed by a Catholic king (497—500); and the remnants of the Roman troops (most of them of barbarian extraction), also acknowledged the sway of Clovis, on condition of their being permitted to retain their arms, their ensigns, and their peculiar dress and institutions.

Clotilda had never ceased to urge her husband to make war upon her uncle, Gundobald, the murderer of her father. Her other uncle, Godegesil, had been permitted by his rapacious brother to retain the dependent principality of Geneva. But fearful lest Gundobald should treat him in the end the same as he had his other brothers, he lent a willing ear to the suggestions of his niece, and the tempting offers of the Frankish king, and entered into a secret compact with the latter to betray and abandon the cause of his brother on the first favourable opportunity. Hereupon Clovis declared war against the King of Burgundy, and invaded his territories: in the year 500 or 501, the armies of the Franks and the Burgundians met between Langres and Dijon. The treacherous desertion, at the decisive moment, of Godegesil and the troops of Geneva, saved Clovis from defeat. Apprehensive of the disaffection of the Gauls, Gundobald abandoned the castle of Dijon, and the important cities of Lyons and Vienna, to the king of the Franks, and continued his flight till he had reached Avignon; but here he made a stand, and defended the city with such skill and vigour, that Clovis ultimately consented to a treaty of peace, which made the King of Burgundy tributary to him, and stipulated the cession of the province of Vienna to Godegesil, as a reward for his treachery.

A garrison of 5000 Franks was left at Vienna, to secure the somewhat doubtful allegiance of Godegesil, and also to protect the latter against the vengeance of his offended brother. But Gundobald, unscrupulous and truculent though he was in the pursuit of his grasping policy, was yet not lacking wisdom. As soon as the conclusion of the peace with Clovis had restored to him the remnant of his kingdom, he applied himself to gain the affections of his Roman and Gallic subjects, by the promulgation of a code of wise and impartial laws, (*lex Gundebalda*— *"La loy Gombette."*—drawn up by Aredius), (502), and to conciliate the Catholic prelates by artful promises of his approaching conversion from the errors of the Arian heresy.

Having strengthened his position, moreover, by alliances with the kings of the Ostrogoths and Visigoths, he suddenly invaded the territories which Clovis had compelled him to cede to his brother, and surprised Vienna and its Frankish garrison ere his brother was even fully aware of his hostile intentions. Godegesil sought refuge in a church; but the protection of the holy precincts availed him nought; he was struck down dead at the altar by his remorseless brother. The provinces of Geneva and Vienna were re-united to the Burgundian kingdom; the captive Franks were sent to the king of the Visigoths, who settled them in the territory of Thoulouse.

Clovis, who could now no longer rely upon the assistance of a traitor in the camp of Gundobald, deemed it the wiser course to submit to the altered state of affairs, and to content himself with the alliance and the promised military service of the King of Burgundy.

Already before the Burgundian war, Clovis had cast his covetous eyes upon the fair provinces of the south of Gaul, which were held by Alaric II, the King of the Visigoths. Here, also, the disaffection of the Catholic Gauls and Romans promised the best chances of success. Some paltry border-squabble was eagerly laid hold of by Clovis to pick a quarrel with the King of

EARLY FRANKISH WARRIOR

the Visigoths, and war seemed at the time inevitable between the two nations; when Theodoric, Alaric's father-in-law, interposed his good offices, and succeeded, by a well-timed threat of an armed intervention, in restraining the aggressive spirit of the Frankish King, (498). (Alaric was married to Theodoric's daughter Theudogotha, or Theodichusa.)

A personal interview was proposed between Clovis and Alaric; it was held on the border of the two states, in a small island of the Loire, near Amboise. The two kings met in right royal fashion: they embraced, feasted together, indulged in a profusion of protestations of mutual regard and brotherly affection, and parted full of smiles—and mutual hatred and distrust.

Had Alaric pursued the same wise course as Gundobald, he might have found in the affection of the people under his sway, a safe shield against Frank aggression. But, unfortunately, the Arian could not forbear from inflicting upon his dissenting subjects, those petty acts of tyranny in which dominant sects delight, and which are always sure to create a deeper and more lasting disaffection than any act of political oppression. The Catholic clergy in Aquitaine laid their complaints against their Arian sovereign, before the Catholic King of the Franks; and besought the latter to come to the aid of his co-religionists, and free them from the yoke of their Gothic tyrants. Clovis eagerly seized the pretext. In a general assembly of the Frankish chiefs and the Catholic prelates held at Paris, he declared his intention not to permit the Arian heretics to retain possession any longer of the fairest portion of Gaul.

Alaric did his best to prepare for the coming struggle; the army which he collected was much more numerous, indeed, than the military power which Clovis could bring against him; but, unfortunately, a long peace had enervated the descendants of the once so formidable warriors of the first Alaric. They were unable to sustain the fierce shock of the Franks, who totally overthrew and routed them in the Battle of Vouglé, near Poitiers, in 507. Alaric himself fell by the hand of his rival; Angoulême, Bordeaux, Thoulouse, submitted to the conqueror, and the whole of Aquitaine acknowledged his sway, (508); and he would have succeeded in driving the Visigoths beyond the Pyrenean mountains, had not the King of Italy thrown the shield of his power over the discomfited nation. The Franks and their Burgundian allies were besieging Arles and Carcassone, when the valiant Hibbas, Theodoric's general, appeared on the scene with a powerful and well-appointed army of Ostrogoths.

He defeated the victors of Vouglé, and compelled the ambitious King of the Franks to raise the siege of the two cities, and to lend a willing ear to proposals of an advantageous peace. He then overthrew and slew the bastard Gesalic, who had usurped the throne of the Visigoths, to the exclusion of Alaric's infant son, Amalaric. The latter was now proclaimed King of Spain and Septimania, under the guardianship of his grandfather, Theodoric: Clovis being permitted to retain possession of the land from the Cevennes and the Garonne to the Loire, whilst the Provence was annexed to the dominions of the King of Italy, who thus did not disdain despoiling his own grandson of one of the finest provinces of his kingdom.

The Emperor Anastasius, overjoyed at the humiliation inflicted by Clovis upon the Goths, bestowed upon the King of the Franks the dignity and ensigns of the Roman consulship! (510); which, though in reality a mere empty title, yet invested that monarch, in the eyes of his Roman and Gallic subjects, with the prestige of Imperial authority.

Clovis seeing himself thus in undisputed possession of the greater part of Gaul, thought the time had come to unite the several Frankish tribes into one nation, under his sceptre. But, knowing full well that his Franks would not follow him in an open war against his own kindred of the race of Pharamond, he coolly planned the assassination of the whole family. Sigebert, the King of the Ripuarians, had proved himself a most faithful ally of his Salian cousin; and in the last campaign against the Visigoths, he had sent to his aid a powerful contingent of his Ripuarians, under the command of his own son, Chloderic.

Clovis excited the ambition and cupidity of the latter, and succeeded in persuading him to murder his own father; when the horrid deed was perpetrated, the wretched son, intent upon securing the powerful support of the Salian king, offered him part of the treasures of the murdered man. The "fair cousin" sent him word to keep his treasures, and simply to show them to his ambassadors, that he, Clovis, might rejoice in the prosperity of his cousin; but, when the assassin of his father had lifted up the heavy lid of one of the boxes, and was bending down to take out some of the precious articles which it held, he was slain in his turn by one of the ambassadors of Clovis. That most Christian king afterwards solemnly protested to the Ripuarians that Chloderic, the assassin of his father, had fallen by the hand of some unknown avenger, and that he, Clovis, was innocent of the death of either of them.

"Surely," he exclaimed, with well affected horror and indignation, "no one would dare to deem me guilty of that most horrible of all crimes, the murder of my own kindred!"

The Ripuarians believed him, and acknowledged him their king, by raising him on a shield. The next victims were Chararic, the King of the Morinic Franks, in Belgium, and his son. Chararic, had refused his aid to Clovis, in the campaign against Syagrius; the fact had, indeed, occurred rather long ago, but still it answered the purpose of the unscrupulous son of Childeric. Chararic and his son, having fallen into his hands by the grossest treachery, were despoiled of their treasures and their long hair, and ordained priests.

When the son, endeavouring to console his father, could not refrain from indignant invectives against the author of their misery, the pious king of the Salians calmly ordered both of them to be slain, as they had "dared to rebel against the will of the Most High!" There remained still the family of the Cambray princes, consisting of three brothers, *viz*., Ragnachar, Richar, and Rignomer. The pretext in their case was that they still continued Pagans. Clovis bribed some of the chiefs of the tribe with spurious gold; they fell unawares upon Ragnachar and Richar, bound them, and delivered them into the hands of their "loving cousin."

Addressing the hapless Ragnachar, that monstrous villain exclaimed, "How dare you bring disgrace upon our noble family, by submitting to the indignity of bonds!" and, with a blow of his battle-axe, he spared the wretched captive the trouble of a reply; then turning to the brother of the butchered man, "Hadst thou defended thy brother," he cried, "they could not have bound him;" and an instant after, the blood and brains of the brothers had mingled their kindred streams on the weapon of the most Christian king. When the wretches who had betrayed their princes into the hands, of the assassin, came to complain that the price of their treachery had been paid in base coin, he told them, traitors deserved no better reward, and bade them be gone, lest he should feel tempted to avenge upon them the blood of his murdered relations.

Rignomer was disposed of by private assassination, and Clovis might now exclaim: "At last I am king of the Franks." The worthy bishop of Tours, the chronicler of this, and some of the following reigns of the Merovingians, whilst coolly relating these horrid crimes of his hero, piously informs us that success in all his undertakings was vouchsafed to Clovis by the Most High, and that his enemies were delivered up into his hands, *because he walked with a sincere heart in the ways of the Lord, and did that which was right in his sight!!* What a pity that this godly monarch was not permitted to walk a little longer in the ways of the Lord: an additional score or so of murders would surely have achieved canonisation for him.

But the most orthodox and most Christian king was suddenly called away from the scene of his glorious exploits; at the very time when he was revolving mighty schemes of further aggrandisement, and planning, as preliminary step, the assassination of Gundobald, the king of Burgundy, and of Theudes, the regent of Spain, (511). His four sons divided his kingdom between them; Theodoric, (Thierry) the eldest, received the Eastern part, Austrasia, (comprised the old Salian possessions in Belgium, and the territories of the Ripuarians and the Alemanni), (*Francia orientalis*), and also part of Champagne, and the conquests of Clovis south of the Loire; he established the seat of his government at Metz; Chlodomir's seat was at Orleans; Clotaire's at Soissons; Childebert's at Paris; the share of the latter was called Neustria or Neustrasia (*Francia occidentalis*), a name which was afterwards used to designate the whole of the territories occupied by the Franks between the mouths of the Rhine and the Loire, the Mouse, and the sea.

It is not my intention to smear these pages with the blood and mire of the lives and acts of the Merovingian princes. We will content ourselves here with a brief glance at the principal events and incidents connected with the progress of the Frank empire during the two hundred years that intervene between the death of Clovis and the accession of Charles, afterwards sur-named Martel, as Mayor of the Palace.

In the year 523, the three sons of Clotilda, invited by their unforgiving mother, invaded Burgundy, and attacked the son and successor of Gundobald, Sigismond, whose conversion to the Catholic faith has gained him, in the lying annals penned by the clerical historians of the period, the name of a saint and a martyr, though he had imbrued his hands in the blood of his own son, an innocent youth whom he had basely sacrificed to the pride of his second wife! Sigismond lost a battle and fell soon after into the hands of the sons of Clotilda, who carried him to Orleans, and had him buried alive together with his wife and two of his children—an excellent proof that they had not *degenerated*. Sigismond's brother, Gondemar, defeated the invaders in the Battle of Vienna, where Clodomir fell. This gave Gondemar a few years' respite, as the two brothers, Clotaire and Childebert, were busy sharing the inheritance of Clodomir.

★★★★★★

Clodomir had left three sons, who were brought up by their grandmother, Clotilda. The two brothers having got possession of two of their nephews, calmly resolved to kill them. Clotaire sheathed his dagger in the breast of one of them, the other embraced the knees of his uncle, Childebert, and besought him to spare his life. The tears of the innocent child moved even the harsh Childebert to pity; he entreated his brother to spare him; but that monster remained deaf to all prayers, and threatened even to make Childebert share the fate of the helpless boy, should he continue any longer to withhold him from his murderous hands: Childebert thereupon pushed back the poor innocent, and Clotaire's dagger speedily sent. him to rejoin his brother (532). The third of the children of Coldomir was, indeed, saved from his uncle's clutches; but he deemed it necessary afterwards to embrace the ecclesiastical profession, in order to secure his safety.

★★★★★★

But, in 534, the brothers invaded Burgundy again; when Gondemar lost his crown and his liberty, and the fair Burgundian provinces became the patrimony of the Merovingian princes. In the year 530, Theodoric and Clotaire conquered and annexed the territories of the Thuringians, thus extending their dominion to the banks of the Unstrut, Rhaetia and Provence also fell into the hands of the successors of Clovis. Theudobald, the grandson and second successor of Theodoric, or Thierry, died in 554; as he left no heir, Clotaire and Childebert shared his dominions between them; Childebert's death, in 558, without male heirs, left Clotaire in sole and undisputed possession of the Frankish empire, which now extended from the Atlantic and the Pyrenees to the Unstrut. After having added to the list of his crimes the murder of his son Chramus, and also of the wife and the two daughters of the latter, King Clotaire died in 560. His kingdom was again divided between his four sons, Charibert, Guntram, Sigebert, and Chilperic; the eldest of the brothers, Charibert, died in 567. As he left no heir, his territories were divided between the three surviving brothers. But Chilperic was dissatisfied with his share, and this led to a series of civil wars, which terminated only in 613, when Clotaire II., the son of Chilperic and Fredegonda, reunited in his hands the entire empire of the Franks.

It would be difficult to crowd a greater number of more appalling and atrocious crimes, within the short space of half a century, than were committed by the Merovingians, from the time of the death of Charibert up to the re-union of the empire under Clotaire II.; the names of Chilperic, of Fredegonda, of Brunehilda, of Theuderic, and last, though not least, of the mon-

61

ster Clotaire (second of the name) deserve, indeed, prominent places in the great criminal calendar of the world's history.

★★★★★★

Fredegonda was first Chilperic's concubine, subsequently, after the murder of Galsuintha, his wife. After a career of blood and crime, of which history affords but few parallels, she died in 579, at the height of prosperity and power, tranquilly in her bed, properly shriven, of course, and with a promise of paradise. Had the female monster been but a little more liberal to the Church, who knows but the Calendar of the Saints might contain an additional name. Brunehilda was the daughter of Athanagild, King of Spain, and the wife of Sigebert, King of Austrasia. She was in every respect a worthy pendant to Fredegonda; but her final fate was very different from that of her more fortunate rival, whom she survived about sixteen years. In the year 613, she fell into the hands of Fredegonda's son, Clotaire, who inflicted upon the aged woman the most horrible tortures, and had her finally tied, with one arm and one leg, to the tail of a wild horse, and thus dragged along over a stony road until death took mercy upon her.

And all these people *professed* the religion of Christ, and were surrounded by numbers of *most pious* bishops! but then, the Church has always been indulgent to those who could and would remember her with rich endowments. Moreover, many of the bishops of that period were themselves such monstrous villains that little or no remonstrance could be expected from them against any royal crime, however so atrocious.—To give one instance out of many: a bishop of Clermont, wishing to compel a priest of his diocese to cede to him a small estate held by the latter, and which he refused to part with, had the unfortunate man shut up in a coffin, with a decaying corpse, and the coffin placed in the vault of the church!

Theuderic, or Thierry, was the younger son of Sigebert's son Childebert; he murdered his elder brother, Theudebert, and the infant son of the latter, Meroveus (612). He died a year after, and two of his own boys, Sigebert and Corbus, met the same fate at the hands of Clotaire.

★★★★★★

THE BATTLE OF TOURS

When the Roman Empire had ceased to exist, the Frankish kings had, in imitation of the Roman rulers, begun to surround themselves with a court, and a great many high officers, and charges had been created, among the most important of which may be mentioned the office of Lord High Chancellor (*archicancellarius, referendarius*); Lord High Chamberlain, or High Treasurer (*thesaurarius, camerarius*); Master of the royal stables (*marescalchus*); Lord Justice (*comes palatii*); Steward of the royal household (*senescalchus*); and more particularly that of Mayor of the Palace (*praefectus palatii*, or *major-domus*, or *comes domûs regiae*). The functions of the latter officer had originally been confined to the general superintendence of the palace, and the administration of the royal domains; but had speedily been extended also to the command of the household troops.

In the course of the domestic wars between the Merovingian princes, the mayors of the palace had gradually acquired a power and influence second only to that of the king; so that, after the assassination of Sigebert, in 575, Gogo, the then mayor of the palace of Austrasia, had actually been named regent during the minority of Sigebert's son, Childebert. So powerful indeed had these domestic officers grown, that Clotaire II. was positively forced to bind himself by oath to Warnachar, the mayor of the palace of Burgundy, to leave him for his life in undisturbed possession of his office; he was obliged also to acknowledge the learned and valiant Arnulf, the Austrasian, mayor of the palace, and subsequently—when that officer embraced the ecclesiastical profession, and became Bishop of Metz—the energetic Pepin of Landen, as his representative with sovereign powers in Austrasia.

★★★★★★

Pepin of Landen was the son of Carloman, a Frank noble of Brabant. Pepin's daughter, Begga, was married to Arnulf's son, Ansgesil; from this marriage sprang Pepin d'Heristal, the father of Charles Martel.

★★★★★★

Even when Clotaire had ceded the kingdom of Austrasia to his son Dagobert (622), Pepin continued to exercise almost unlimited sway in that part of the Frankish empire. After Clotaire's death, in 623, Dagobert succeeded also to the Neustrian kingdom; and in 631, after his brother Charibert's death, who had held some of the south-western provinces, he became sole king of France.

★★★★★★

However, two natural sons of Charibert founded, after the death of the latter, the semi-independent duchy of Aquitaine, in a more restricted sense, with the capital, Thoulouse.

★★★★★★

He died in 638; he was a compound of sensuality and indolence; still his character and life were not stained with the horrible crimes perpetrated by his predecessors, and more particularly by his own father; he was the last of the descendants of Clevis, who exhibited even the faintest spark of that fierce and energetic spirit which made the founder of the Frank monarchy, however so abhorrent as a man, yet respectable, and even great, as a king, Dagobert built and richly endowed the Church of St. Denys, which gained him the surname "The Great," from a grateful clergy; but history has refused to register the ill-deserved epithet. Pepin of Landen died a year after his king (639).

His son, Grimoald, deemed the power of his family already so firmly established, that, taking advantage of the tender age of Dagobert's sons, Sigebert (second of the name in the list of the Merovingian kings), and Clovis (II.), he attempted to deprive them of their father's succession, and to place his own son (Childebert) on the throne; both father and son paid with their lives the failure of the ambitious plan. But the overthrow of Grimoald led simply to a change of persons; the power of the mayors of the palace remained undiminished, and from this time forward, the Merovingian kings were mere ciphers. "They ascended the throne without power, and sunk into the grave without a name."

(Gibbon.)

Sigebert died in 650; his brother Clovis six years after. One of the sons of the latter, Clotaire (III.), succeeded to the Neustrian, another, Childeric (II.), to the Austrasian part of the empire. After Clotaire's death, in 670, the third brother, Theodoric, or Thierry (III.), was for a short time King of Neustria; but he was speedily dispossessed by his brother Childeric (or to speak more correctly, *his* mayor of the palace was compelled to give way to Childeric's mayor of the palace). Childeric was murdered in 673; when Thierry was reinstated in Neustria, Austrasia being given to Dagobert (II.), a son of Sigebert II., but who had hitherto been kept out of his inheritance.

After the death of Dagobert in 678, the Austrasians refused to submit to Thierry, the King of Neustria and Burgundy, or rather to his haughty mayor of the palace, Ebroin. Pepin d'Heristal, the grandson of Pepin of Landen, and his cousin, Martin, were at the head of the insurgent Austrasian nobility. Martin fell into the hands of Ebroin, and was killed. Ebroin himself was soon after assassinated, (682). His successor, Giselmar, defeated Pepin at Namur, but the Austrasian notwithstanding maintained his position. The Neustrian nobility, discontented with the rule of Giselmar's successor, Berthar or Berchar, ultimately called Pepin to their aid.

Berthar, and his puppet, Thierry, were defeated by the Austrasian ruler in the famous Battle of Testry, near Peronne and St. Quentin, in 687. Berthar was slain as he fled from the field of battle: and although the name of king was left to Thierry, he was compelled to acknowledge Pepin as *sole*, *perpetual*, and *hereditary* Mayor of the Palace, in the three kingdoms of Neustria, Austrasia, and Burgundy, under the style and title of Duke and Prince of the Franks, (*Dux et Princeps Francorum*). Pepin was now, to all intents and purposes, the actual ruler of the Frankish empire— king in all but the name.

The nominal sovereigns had, henceforth, a residence assigned them, Mamaccae (Mommarques) on the Oise between Compiègne and Noyon, which they dared not even quit without the sanction of their master; nay, even the paltry consolation of the pomp and glitter of royalty was not vouchsafed them—except once a year in the month of March, when the royal puppet was conducted in state in the old Frankish fashion, in a waggon drawn by two oxen, to the great annual assembly of the nation; to give audience to foreign ambassadors, or to receive plaints and petitions—and to place his organ of speech, for a time, at the disposal of the Mayor of the Palace, and give utterance to the replies or decisions of the real ruler of France.

★★★★★★

Pepin of Heristal restored the annual national assembly of the Franks, which had fallen in desuetude since the days of Ebroin; when the younger Pepin, the son of Charles Martel, finally added the name of King to the exercise of the royal power which he yielded, he changed the month of meeting from March to May; the *Campus Martius* became accordingly a *Campus Majus,*

★★★★★★

The assembly over, the "King" was reconducted to his residence or prison, where a feeble retinue and a strong guard insulted the fallen majesty of the house of Clovis. It would even appear, that the civil list assigned to the "King," was only a precarious grant, and that the nominal master of three kingdoms, was often left without the means of defraying the expenses of his humble household. The epithet of the "do-nothing kings," (*les rois fainéans*) has been felicitously applied to the last princes of the Merovingian line. Besides Thierry III, (+ 621), three of them lived in the reign of Pepin of Heristal, *viz*: Clovis III, (+ 695); Childebert III, (+ 711); and Dagobert III., all of them minors.

Pepin was an able and energetic ruler; he restored in some measure the respect of the law. Liberal Rewards secured him the allegiance of the nobility; munificent endowments to churches and monasteries, and the aid and encouragement which he gave to the Christian missionaries, who were endeavouring to convert the heathen Germans, gained him the favour and support of the clergy: his good sword put down the discontented; and last, though certainly not least, he deserved the grateful affection of the people by alleviating their burthens, and by protecting them, in some measure, against the despotic oppression of the nobility.

The expulsion of some Christian missionaries from Friesland, gave Pepin a pretext for endeavouring to subject the Frisons to the Frankish sway. He invaded Friesland in 689, and defeated the Frison duke, or prince, Radbodus, at Dorestadt, or Dorsted; in consequence of which defeat, the latter was compelled to cede West Friesland to the Duke of the Franks; but all attempts to obtain the conversion of Radbodus to Christianity failed.

★★★★★★

At one time, it would appear, the Frison prince was on the point of consenting to his baptism; he had already placed one foot in the baptismal font, when it occurred to him to ask the officiating bishop (Wolfram, of Sens), "where his ancestors were gone to?" "To Hell," was the unhesitating reply of the bigoted priest; whereupon the honest heathen exclaimed: "Then I will rather be damned with them than saved without them," and withdrew his foot.

★★★★★★

In 697, a new war broke out between the Duke of the Franks and the Prince of the Frisons, (perhaps in some measure in consequence of the consecration of the missionary, Willibrod, as bishop of Utrecht, 696), in which the latter is stated to have been again defeated, and compelled to acknowledge, by the payment of an annual tribute, the supremacy of the Franks. It is added, also, that he gave his daughter in marriage to Pepin's son Grimoald.

Pepin of Heristal made also several expeditions, though, it would appear, with indifferent success only, against the Alemanni, the Thuringians, and the Bojoarii, or Bavarians, who had taken advantage of the internal dissensions and disorder of the Frankish empire, to shake off the yoke of their masters.

In the beginning of the year 714, Pepin fell seriously ill, at his estate Jopila, on the Meuse. He sent for his only surviving (legitimate) son, Grimoald, whom he had made (after the death of his friend Nordbert) *major domus* in Neustria, and (after the death of Drogo, another of his sons) Duke of Burgundy and Champagne, and whom he intended to name his successor in the government of the entire monarchy. But on his way to his father, Grimoald was assassinated at Liège, in the church of St. Lambert, by a Frison; at the instigation, it would appear, of some discontented nobles.

He left an illegitimate infant son, Theudoald, or Theudebaud. Pepin was unfortunately persuaded by his wife, the ambitious Plectrudis, (of the race of the Bojoarian Agilolfingians), who expected to wield the government during the minority of her little grandson, to name this infant his successor, instead of either of his own two illegitimate sons (Charles and Childebrand), (Alpais, or Alpheida, was the mother of these two sons), and of whom the latter, more especially, possessed his father's great qualities, and that amount of physical and intellectual vigour indispensable to keep together and to rule over an empire composed of such heterogeneous and antagonistic elements, as the Frankish.

Soon after this fatal step, which, we may safely assume the love of his country and of his glory, would never have permitted the aged ruler to take, had not his faculties been greatly impaired at the time by long illness and by the bitter grief of his son's death, Pepin of Heristal died on the 16th of December, 714.

He had scarcely departed life when Plectrudis, who dreaded the aspiring genius of Charles, had the latter seized, and confined in the city of Cologne. She now deemed herself in safe possession of the government; but she was soon awakened from her ambitious dream. The Neustrians were indignant that they should thus be handed over to the sway of a child and to the rule of a woman: they could bear infant-kings, indeed, but they refused to put up with an infant mayor of the palace. They, therefore, made Raganfried, a powerful Neustrian noble, their mayor of the palace, and prepared to resist by force of arms, any attempt which Plectrudis might make to compel their submission. The widow of Pepin showed indeed that, if she had had the ambition to seize the sceptre, she had also the spirit to wield, and the requisite energy to defend it.

She collected a powerful army, and sent the puppet-King Dagobert (III.)? and his infant minister Theudebaud, with it against, what she was pleased to call, the Neustrian rebels. But the fortune of war declared against her: the Austrasian forces were totally routed by Raganfried, and "King" Dagobert fell into the hands of the Neustrian mayor of the palace. The infant on whose tiny shoulders Pepin's ill-judged partiality, or uxoriousness, had thrown the burthen of three kingdoms, died soon after this reverse (715).

Radbodus took advantage of the position of affairs, to re-annex West Friesland to his dominions; and, in conjunction with the Saxons, invaded the Frankish territories from the north east, whilst the Merovingian princes of Aquitaine ravaged them in the south west; the Alemanni and the Bavarians threw off the Frankish yoke, and resumed their ancient independence. Matters were looking dark indeed for the house of the Pepins, and though Mistress Plectrudis most gallantly braved the storm, her utmost efforts could have availed but little against such a multitude of foes, had not Pepin's son, Charles, meanwhile found his way out of the prison to which the ambition of his father's widow had confined him.

Charles, who was destined afterwards to play so important a part in history, was, at this time, about 25 years of age (he was born in 690). Nature had been most bountiful to him: tall even among the tall nation of the Franks, of a most commanding figure, and of a compact and beautifully symmetrical frame, he might be said to present in his physical conformation a compound of Hercules and Antinous; his features were regular and expressive, and the lightning glance of his large blue eyes reflected, as in a mirror, the energy of his mind and the vigour of his intellect. He possessed enormous bodily strength combined with surprising agility.

The remembrance of his great father, and his own manly beauty, and grace, gained him the hearts of the Austrasians; and he soon found himself at the head of a formidable body of troops, with which he proceeded first to attack the Frisons, but with rather indifferent success, it would appear, as, we find Radbodus and his Frisons soon after laying siege to Cologne, in conjunction with the Neustrians under Raganfried. Plectrudis, however, purchased the retreat of the besieging forces; and the Prisons and Neustrians having separated again, Charles fell upon the latter at Ambleva. But, although he exhibited all the qualities of a great general, and that the fearful execution which his heavy sword did in the hostile ranks struck terror into the foe, and made ever after his war-cry "Here Charles and his sword," ring as the prelude of inevitable defeat on the affrighted ears of his enemies: yet the superiority of numbers was too great on the side of Raganfried, and the battle terminated at last rather in favour of the Neustrians than otherwise (716).

Soon after his capture by the Neustrians, Dagobert had passed from his royal prison to the grave (715), and another unlucky scion of the race of Pharamond, the Monk Daniel, had been dragged from the repose of his cloistral cell, to figure, as Chilperic II., in the line of the " titular" kings of France. Charles would have acquiesced in the arrangement, had not Raganfried steadily refused to acknowledge him as Duke of Austrasia; he determined, therefore, to appeal once more to the decision of arms. A fierce and sanguinary battle was fought between the Austrasians and the Neustrians, at Vincy, between Arras and Cambray (21st of March, 717): and this time, Charles' valour and generalship were rewarded with a brilliant and decisive victory, which made him master of the country up to Paris.

But, wisely declining to pursue his conquests in this quarter, and to court perhaps the chance of a defeat far away from his resources, he led his victorious army swiftly back to the Rhine, and compelled Plectrudis to give up to him the city of Cologne, and his paternal treasures; which latter he turned to excellent account in increasing the number and efficiency of his forces. Plectrudis took refuge in Bavaria.

Though the Merovingian princes had lost all real power in the state, yet there still attached to the name of the family a prestige in the eyes of the nation, which rendered the continued existence of "Kings" chosen from among the descendants of Clovis, a matter of political necessity. Charles wisely resolved therefore, to put himself in this respect on equal terms with Raganfried; and he accordingly invested with the insignia of a sham royalty another scion of the long-haired line, yclept Clotaire, fourth of that name. An expedition against the Saxons, to chastise them for their predatory incursions into the Frankish territories, was eminently successful, and the son of Pepin displayed his victorious banner on the Weser (718); but receiving information that Raganfried had made an alliance against him with the valiant Eudes, Duke of Aquitaine (of Merovingian descent), and dreading lest the united power of the two might prove too strong for him, he resolved to attack the former before a junction of the allied forces could be effected, and accordingly led his army with his accustomed celerity from the banks of the Weser to the banks of the Seine. After totally routing Raganfried at Soissons (719), he compelled Paris to surrender. The wretched Chilperic, (Raganfried had most likely perished on his flight), sought refuge with his ally, Eudes.

Charles marched on to the Loire, and was preparing to carry his arms into Aquitaine, when the death of Clotaire led to an arrangement with Chilperic, who, acknowledging Charles as *major domus* in the three kingdoms, was permitted to continue in the enjoyment of his fictitious royalty. In the same year still (719), Charles was delivered by death from another of his opponents, Radbodus, the brave duke of the Frisons. He promptly took advantage of this event to re-annex West Friesland to the Frankish dependencies, and to induct Bishop Willibrod into his see of Utrecht, from which Radbodus had kept him excluded.

In the year 720, Chilperic was gathered to his fathers; Charles replaced him by a child of the Merovingian race, taken from the monastery of Lala (Thierry IV). In 721 Charles crossed the Rhine at the head of a powerful army, to subject the Alemanni, the Bavarians, and the Thuringians again to the Frankish sway. As he saw in the conversion of these stubborn nations to Christianity one of the most efficient means to secure their allegiance in future, he had himself attended by Winifried, and other missionaries, who, now that they were supported by the arms of the Frankish chief, were brilliantly successful in their missionary labours, in some of the very places among others, where they had on former occasions been treated with derision and contumely, or whence they had been forcibly expelled.

★★★★★★

Winifried, better known as Boniface, the Apostle of the Germans. He was sent by Charles to Rome to obtain the episcopal ordination, that he might be able to act with greater ecclesiastical authority in the newly converted districts; on the 30th November, 723, Pope Gregory II. (715—731) ordained him bishop, after he had given in his "profession of faith," which was approved of by Gregory as strictly orthodox.

The pope furnished him then with letters and credentials to Christian princes and ecclesiastics, and to the heathen princes and nations of Germany, and also with faithful copies of the ordinances, creed, ritual, and regulations of the Romish Church; and the Christian missionary was thus converted into the Popish legate. By his base monkish truckling to the authority of Rome this narrow-minded zealot, who sought in idle formalities and ceremonies the *spirit* of the word of Christ, which he was totally unable to conceive and comprehend, turned the new Christian church in Germany into a dependence of the Papal see, and thus prepared ages of bloodshed and misery for that devoted country.

He carried his "submissiveness" to Rome so far that he actually asked instructions in that quarter as to whether, on which part of the body, and with which finger he might, or was to, make the sign of the cross during the delivery of his sermons. No wonder, indeed, his "mission" succeeded only when backed by the sword. He was murdered by the Frisons, in 765. Apart from his narrow-minded bigotry, he was an estimable man, full of honest and disinterested zeal.

★★★★★★

In 722, Charles drove the Saxons from the Hassian (Hessian) district which they had invaded; but when he followed them into their own country, with the intention of subjecting them altogether to his sway, he experienced such determined resistance that he wisely resolved to leave them alone. In 725, he compelled the Suabians and Alemanni, and their duke, Lantfried, to acknowledge his sovereignty.

Since 553, after the extinction of the Gothic kingdom of Italy, the Agilolfingian dukes of Bavaria "enjoyed" the "protection" of the Frankish kings; although, whenever the dissensions among the members of that amiable family, or the contentions among the mayors of the palace, afforded a fitting opportunity, the Bavarians invariably took occasion to "thank" them for their protection, and to decline further favours.

★★★★★★

The ingenuity displayed by man in the invention of specious terms to disguise the plain and simple fact of the domination of one being or nation over another, is truly marvellous.

★★★★★★

But the persuasive force of Pepin of Heristal, and of his son Charles, fully succeeded in the end in restoring the amicable relations between the two nations, to the old footing. Duke Theodo II., a most pious prince, who greatly favoured and furthered the extension of Christianity in his dominions, committed the capital blunder so common at the time (and so natural withal)—to divide his dominions between his three sons, Theodoald (Theudebaud), Theudebert, and Grimoald. Theudebaud had married Pilitrudis, the fair daughter of Plectrudis; he died in 716, and his brother Grimoald deemed it no harm to marry the beautiful widow of the departed; but Saint Corbinian happened to think very differently; and his zealous exhortations, and the fearful picture which he drew of the pains and penalties that awaited him who should have committed, what the holy man was pleased to call, "incest," frightened poor Duke Grimoald into giving his consent to a divorce from his dearly beloved wife. (What a blessing a Primate like St. Corbinian would have been to the tender-conscienced casuist, Henry VIII, of England.)

Mistress Pilitrudis, however, was by no means pleased with the pusillanimous conduct of her second husband; and the exile of the meddlesome ecclesiastic speedily showed him, that a woman offended may prove more than a match *even* for a priest

73

and a saint. Theudebert also died (724), leaving behind a son, named Hugibert, and a daughter, named Guntrudis, and who was married to Liutprand, King of the Lombards. After his second brother's death, Grimoald seized upon his dominions to the prejudice of his nephew. Hugibert, finding all his remonstrances disregarded, claimed the intercession of the Duke of the Franks, in his capacity as Protector of Bavaria.

Charles accepted the offer of mediator between the contending parties; and called upon Grimoald to deliver up to Hugibert the provinces which he was unjustly withholding from him. Grimoald refusing, Charles entered Bavaria at the head of his army, and the Bavarian duke was defeated and slain in the first battle (725). Hugibert now succeeded to the government of all Bavaria, (of course, under Frankish protection), with the exception, however, of a large slice of the Northern provinces, which he ceded to Charles in reward of his services. (Or as the dower of Suanehilda, Theudebaud's daughter of a former marriage, whom Charles espoused on this occasion.)

The unfortunate Pilitrudis was despoiled by the "magnanimous" victor of all she possessed, except a mule, or donkey, to carry her to Pavia to her relations. A new irruption of the Saxons, called Charles again to the Weser; he defeated and drove back the invaders (729). Whilst he was thus occupied on the Saxon frontier, the Suabians and Alemanni took advantage of his absence, to throw off once more the yoke of the Franks. Charles confounded them, however, by the rapidity of his movements; he appeared on the Mein before they were well aware that he had left the banks of the Weser. The battle which ensued, terminated in the total defeat of the "rebels;" Duke Lantfried. was slain, and the humbled nation submitted to the rule of the conqueror (730).

We are now approaching the most important and most interesting period in the life and career of Charles, *viz.*, his encounter with the Saracens; we will, therefore, resume here the thread of the history of the Moslem invasion, broken off where we left the Saracen general. El Zama, laying siege to Thoulouse. A branch of the Merovingian family, descended from Clotaire's (II.) younger son Charibert (631), had established the independent, (virtually independent), duchy of Aquitaine in the south of France. At the time of the Arab invasion, Eudes (Eudo, or Odo), an able and energetic prince, was Duke of Aquitaine. This prince, seeing his capital threatened by the Moslems, collected a numerous army of Gascons, Goths, and Franks, and marched bravely to the rescue.

He attacked the Arabs under the walls of Thoulouse, and succeeded in inflicting on them a most disastrous defeat (721). El Zama fell in the battle, and the discomfited Moslems were saved from total destruction only by the prudence and valour of Abdalrahman Ben Abdallah (Abderrahman, or Abderame), a veteran officer, whom they had elected by acclamation in the place of their late general.

The *Khalif*, however, did not ratify the choice of the army, but named Anbesa to the government of Spain. The new governor advanced again into Aquitaine in 725; he took Carcassone by storm, and penetrated as far as Burgundy; but the valiant Eudes succeeded ultimately in driving him back, and also in defeating several subsequent attempts of the Arabs to gain possession of Aquitaine.

In the year 730, the Khalif Hesham, yielding to the wishes of the people and the army of Spain, restored Abdalrahman to the government of that part of the Arab dominions. That daring and ambitious commander proposed to subject to his sway, not only Aquitaine, but the entire Frank empire; and collected a formidable host to carry his resolve into execution. But, at the very threshold of his enterprise, he met with an obstacle which, though he indeed triumphantly overcame it, yet cannot be denied to have exercised a powerful adverse influence upon its final issue. This was the rebellion of Othman, or Munuza, a Moorish chief, who, as governor of Cerdagne, held the most important passes of the Pyrenees.

The fortune of war had placed the beauteous daughter of Eudes in the hands of Munuza; and the political Duke of Aquitaine, justly appreciating the advantages of an alliance with the man who might be said to hold the keys of his house, had willingly consented to accept the African misbeliever for his son-in-law. The skill, rapidity, and decision, of Abdalrahman's movements undoubtedly disconcerted the strategic combinations of the two allies, and Munuza was overcome and slain, ere Eudes could hasten to his assistance; the head of the rebel, and the daughter of the Duke of Aquitaine, were sent to Damascus. But much precious time was consumed, and a great number of combatants were lost, in this unexpected prelude to the invasion of France. However, immediately after the overthrow of Munuza, Abdalrahman advanced rapidly to the Rhone, crossed that river, and laid siege to Aries; Eudes attempted to relieve the beleaguered city, but his army was totally routed, and Aries fell into the hands of the invaders (731).

Abdalrahman speedily conquered the greater part of Aquitaine, and advanced to Bordeaux. The intrepid Eudes met him once more, at the head of a numerous army; but neither the valour and skill of the Christian leader nor the bravery of his troops could save them from a most disastrous defeat. Bordeaux fell, and the Saracens overran the fairest provinces of France (732). Charles, who would most probably have remained deaf to the most urgent entreaties of Eudes, whom he regarded in the light of a rival, comprehended the necessity of a speedy and vigorous action, from the moment that he saw his own dominions threatened.

He, therefore, rapidly collected his faithful Austrasians and the auxiliary contingents of the Alemanni, the Thuringians, and the Bavarians; and ordered the Neustrian and Burgundian nobles to join him with their followers; and although many of the Burgundian nobles hung back, yet a most powerful host of the nations of Germany and Gaul gathered under the banner of the Christian leader, who was joined also by Eudes and the remains of the Aquitanian Army. In the centre of France, between Tours and Poitiers, the Franks and the Moslems met, in the month of October, 732. Six days were spent in desultory warfare, and many a gallant heart had ceased to beat, ere as the red sun of the seventh day rose, the day on which it was to be decided whether mosque or cathedral should prevail in Europe.

The battle raged fiercely from noon till eventide; the fiery sons of the South fought with tenfold their accustomed valour, and Abdalrahman emulated the glory of Kaled "the Sword of God." The Germans stood firm as rocks, and fought as heroes; and the heavy battle-axe of Charles, wielded with irresistible strength, spread death and dismay in the Arabian ranks; the mighty strokes which the Christian hero dealt with that formidable weapon, gained him the epithet of *Martel*, the *Hammer*. Eudes, burning with the resentment of former defeats, strove to rival the prowess of his ally. Still, for many hours, the balance hung equipoised. The life-blood of thousands of Christians and thousands of Moslems, that had ere just raced so fiercely through its channels, mingled in sluggish streams on the ground.

Evening set in, and still the contest rage with unabated fury; the Orientals had, indeed, repeatedly been forced to give way to the superior weight and strength of the Germans but their heroic chief had as often rallied them and led them on again to death and glory. At length, a German spear struck him to death: his fall decided the fate of the battle; the Saracens, disheartened by the loss of their great commander, retired to their camp.

There was no leader left among them of sufficient renown and authority to replace the fallen hero; despairing of their ability to renew the fight next day with the slightest chance of success, they resolved upon a hasty retreat; and taking with them the richest and most portable portion of their spoil, they abandoned their camp in the middle of the night.

Next morning, when Charles was marshalling forth his troops to renew the contest, his spies both surprised and rejoiced him with the welcome intelligence that the enemy were in full retreat to the south. The victory gained was decisive and final: the torrent of Arabian conquest was rolled back; and Europe was rescued from the threatened yoke of the Saracens. But the losses of the Christians also had been very great, and Charles wisely declined incurring with his sadly diminished forces, the possible mischances of a pursuit.

★★★★★★

The idle and incredibly extravagant tale told by Paul

ABDUL–AL–RAHMAN

Warnefried and Anastasius of 350,000 or 375,000 Arabs slain in this battle, to 1500 Christians, has been faithfully copied by most historians. One should think a moment's reflection would suffice to show the absolute impossibility of these numbers. Where on earth was a governor of Spain, a recent conquest of the Saracens, to find the 450,000 men (for 100,000 are stated to have escaped) to lead into France; and where was he to find, in a thinly populated region, such as that country was in the time of Charles Martel, the means of subsistence for such a host? His chief of the commissariat must have been a rare genius indeed. And as to the number of *fifteen hundred* Christians slain, this looks very much like the "one man killed and four men slightly wounded," to "one thousand of the enemy slain," of some of our modern bulletins. Striking off a nought from the number of the Saracens, and adding one to that of the Christians may bring us somewhat nearer the truth.

★★★★★★

Leaving to Eudes the task of reconquering his own land from the flying foe, Charles proceeded now to call the Burgundian nobles to account for their hesitation and lukewarmness in his cause. To secure their future allegiance, he placed officers of his into the Burgundian cities and castles; to little purpose, however, it would appear, as their presence did not prevent the discontented Burgundian nobles, a few years after, from calling in the Saracens, and actually delivering the city of Avignon into the hands of Jussuf Ben Abdalrahman, the Arabian governor of Narbonne (735).

In 734, Charles defeated Poppo, the Duke of the Frisons, and regained the western part of Friesland. In 735, Duke Eudes died, and as his two sons, Hunold and Hatto, quarrelled about the succession, Charles proffered his "armed mediation," and settled the dispute finally by naming Hunold Duke of Aquitaine, after having exacted and obtained from that prince an oath of allegiance, not to the nominal king of the Franks, but to himself personally, and to his two sons of his first marriage, Carloman and Pepin. In

736, Charles had to repel another invasion of the Saxons, which prevented him from proceeding to Burgundy against the disaffected nobles and their allies, the Arabs; he sent, however, his brother Childebrand.

In 737, he came himself; he speedily reduced Avignon, and expelled the Arabs from the Burgundian territory; the nobility and clergy, who had treasonably conspired against him with the enemy, or had acted in a hostile manner to him, he deprived of their possessions, bishoprics, &c., which he bestowed upon his friends and followers.

★★★★★★

Charles Martel was not over-nice, it would appear, in the bestowal of ecclesiastical preferments and estates; it mattered very little indeed to him whether the recipient was a priest or a layman, or even whether he could read and write. He also laid his impious hands repeatedly upon the revenues of the church, and applied them to the necessities of the state, or to pay his soldiers. No wonder then that a sainted bishop of the times, Eucherius, of Orleans, should have been indulged with a pleasant vision of the body and soul of the wicked prince burning in the deepest abyss of hell—rather scurvy treatment, though, on the part of a Christian clergy, of a prince who, whatever might be his foibles as a man, and his vices as a king—(and it must be admitted, he had a goodly share of them)—had yet the merit of being the saviour of Christendom. (A synod held at Quiercy, in 858, had the calm impudence to communicate this interesting and flattering statement, accompanied by some others of the same stamp, to Lewis, King of Germany, grandson of Charlemagne!)

★★★★★★

In 738 he advanced into Septimania, and laid siege to Narbonne. He totally defeated Omar Ben Kaled, the Arabian general, who was marching to the relief of the beleaguered city; but the governor of Narbonne defended the place so valiantly and successfully, that the Franks were compelled to raise the siege. However, though Septimania remained in the hands of the Arabs till 755, when Pepin, the son of Charles Martel, recovered it, an effectual and final check had been put to their further advance into France.

In 737, King Thierry died; but so firmly was the power of Charles Martel established now, that he could safely neglect to name a successor to the dead "monarch;" nay, in 741, he actually proceeded before a general assembly of the nobility and the army, to divide his dominions between his two sons of his first marriage (with Rotrudis), bestowing Austrasia, with Suabia and Thuringia, upon the elder, Carloman; Neustria, Burgundy, and Provence, upon the younger, Pepin. His son Grypho, whom Suanehilda had borne him, he excluded at first from all participation in his succession; subsequently he assigned him also a portion, which, after his death, led to the oppression and imprisonment of the youth by his elder brothers. In the same year (741) Charles was, on his return from a kind of pilgrimage to St. Denys, seized with a violent fever, of which he died at Carisiacum, or Quiercy, on the Oise, on the 22nd October.

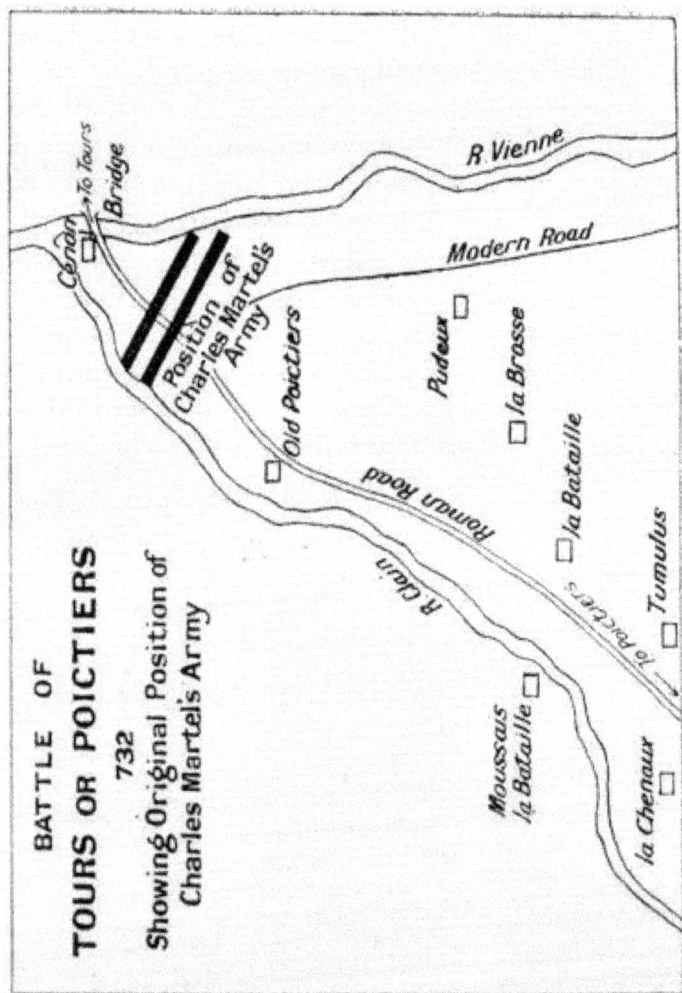

BATTLE OF

TOURS OR POICTIERS

732

Showing Original Position of
Charles Martel's Army

R. Vienne

Modern Road

To Tours

Cenon

Bridge

Position of
Charles Martel's
Army

Old Poictiers

Roman Road

R. Clain

To Poictiers

Pideux

la Brasse

la Bataille

Tumulus

Moussais
la Bataille

la Chenaur

Tours, 732 A. D.

By Charles King

For years after the Battle of Châlons, *A.D.* 451, great changes were taking place in Christendom. The Roman Empire died out in the West. The Saxons and Angles conquered Britain. Italy and Northern Africa were for a time added to the Roman Empire of the East. Wars were vigorously carried on between the Emperors of Constantinople and the Kings of Persia well into the seventh century. Then came the era of Mohammed and the Hegira, in 622. Then Mohammed conquered Arabia, and during the remainder of the century the Mohammedan Arabs, gaining constantly in strength and confidence, invaded first Persia, then conquered Syria, Egypt and Africa; and early in the eighth century, from 707 to 713, they had crossed the straits of Gibraltar, and were battling and conquering all over Spain.

The Germanic conquerors of Rome had, three centuries before this, fallen back across the Rhine, never to return. A French monarchy had been founded in Gaul by King Clovis, and for three hundred years it had struggled on. Now, the peace, prosperity and the hopes of Christian France were threatened by this advancing wave of followers of the prophet. Everywhere, from the south of Gaul, along Africa, Egypt, Arabia, Syria, far to Eastern Persia, everywhere, from the Pyrenees to the Himalayas, the name of Mohammed was worshipped, and his *Koran* was the law.

And now, with a veteran and united army, thoroughly disciplined and equipped, these determined Saracens had planted their magazines along the frontier and with stores in abundance, with every advantage in their favour, they were about to cross the Pyrenees and attempt the conquest of Gaul. From Persia to Spain the Caliph was the supreme power, and him the Moslems obeyed unhesitatingly; and his trusted general, Abderrahman Abdillah Alghafeki, was governor in Spain and commander of the army of occupation. Abderrahman was the hero of the Saracen soldiery, a tried leader, a generous and zealous man, and it was with unbounded confidence that they prepared to follow him across the mountains to the plains of Southern France.

In the summer of 732, at the head of 80,000 soldiers, among whom were some admirable Arabian cavalry, Abderrahman crossed the Pyrenees as Hannibal had crossed them ten centuries before, and swooped down upon the cities and towns that lay before him. France had no army with which to successfully oppose him. Count Eudes, of Aquitaine, strove to check him on the Garonne, but was beaten with great loss, and beyond doubt the Mohammedan invasion of France would have been a complete success, had the leading men not promptly called to their aid Prince Charles, of the Austrasian Franks, over near the Rhine; and this Charles, surnamed Martel (the Hammer), lost no time in pushing forward with his irregular cavalry to join forces with his western neighbours, and, just one hundred years after the death of Mohammed, the followers of the prophet were met and overthrown in "the deadly Battle" of Tours.

More than one great fight has taken place in the beautiful valley of the Loire, but none has the historic interest which centres in this. Great, decisive and important as was the annihilation of the *legions* of Varus by the German Arminius, the victory of Charles Martel over the Saracens at Tours outrivalled it in national consequence. Doctor Arnold, the eminent English writer of history, regards the latter as the most important and decisive of the middle ages. It was the check to Mohammedan invasion, without which Southwestern Europe would have been overrun as was South-eastern, where, to this day, (1884), the descendants of the Saracens are the rulers of Turkey, the holders of the great city which Napoleon described as "the Empire of the World."

Charles Martel had no standing army, but years of warfare

The Hammer of Christendom

had skilled his hand and eye, and given strength to his own high courage. He organised a large force of militia among the Franks, and brought with him, to the rescue of his kinsmen, a considerable body of horse and foot from along the Rhine. Just how many men he could muster nobody seems to know. The historians of that day were the old monks, who wrote very vaguely when it came to describing military matters, nor were the accounts on the Saracen side any more complete.

From all obtainable sources it would seem that, after crossing the Pyrenees and defeating Count Eumenes on the Garonne, the 80,000 soldiery of Abderrahman scattered over the level plains of France, robbing, burning and destroying in a most ruthless manner. It is related by the monks that so sure were they of success and of subduing the whole country, that it appeared as though this Moslem Army of occupation had come to stay permanently, for they brought with them their wives and children, flocks and herds, and all their belongings. It was an invasion with a purpose.

Abderrahman had obtained accurate information as to the real inhabitants, their means of defence, etc., and knew that from them he had nothing to dread. Of Charles Martel and the possibility of interference where he was concerned, he had apparently little idea. His army was allowed to scatter in every direction over the broad, fertile valleys, and in so doing they became necessarily disorganised, and lost much of their discipline. Their Berber or Arabian light cavalry committed terrible ravages throughout the land, and the bitterest hatred sprang up against them. Whatever the Franks were lacking in warlike instruction they soon made up in eager daring; and, taking advantage of their ardour and the scattered condition of the Saracens, Martel probably wisely chose to strike hard and quick, without even waiting to organise and discipline his volunteers.

The armies met near the city of Tours, on the broad River Loire. The invaders had already assaulted the walls and were carrying everything before them—even committing the greatest excesses and crimes. While thus plunder-laden, and scattered and disordered, the army of Martel marched steadily down upon them. Abderrahman hastily recalled his forces and strove to form lines, and several days of indecisive skirmishing passed by. His Arabian cavalry, always ready and daring, opened the real battle on the 3rd of October, charging again and again upon the sturdily advancing lines of the Franks, inflicting great losses but suffering severely on their own side.

Martel had but few horsemen to oppose to such trained riders as these, and for some time it seemed as though their wild attacks must succeed in wearing out the firmness of the soldiers of Gaul, unused as they had long been to anything like warfare; but Martel was spirited, hopeful and energetic, fighting cautiously but bravely, and when at last the day was done he had succeeded in engaging the entire host of Abderrahman; had compelled him to abandon the assault of the city in the moment of triumph, and in holding his own position intact against the furious charges of the enemy. The first day closed decidedly in his favour, and Abderrahman was driven into his camp, to the south towards Poictiers.

But the battle was not yet won. At the first grey of dawn the Moslem cavalry were at them again, but now the awe they had inspired in the breasts of the simple-minded peasantry had disappeared. The Franks had gained great confidence, and not only repulsed the charges with heavy loss, but soon began to press the squadrons in retreat and force them in turn. It so happened therefore that a cry went up that the camp in rear of Abderrahman's lines was being attacked, and all the plunder would be recaptured. This added to the unsteadiness of the troops already shaken by the determined stand of the Franks, Dozens of squadrons broke, galloping off to the rear under pretence of defending the camp.

The lines of Abderrahman began to waver. He himself was quick to note it and to throw himself into the thick of the fight, calling on all to stand by him; but Martel, too, with a soldier's keen eye, had marked every symptom, and now at last ordered a general advance and charge upon the Saracens. With one simultaneous impulse the Frankish Army swept forward; Abderrahman, fighting like a lion, was surrounded, hewed down and pierced by a dozen spears. Then indeed the demoralised army could stand it no longer and broke and fled closely and vehemently pursued. Martel, like Caesar, gave no rest to beaten foe; no time to rally and try it again. Everywhere the Moslems were cut down and slaughtered, for no mercy was shown to those who had been so unmerciful, and the carnage during that long afternoon of pursuit was something indescribable.

One writer of the day asserts that over 300,000 Saracens were slain, and that the loss of Charles Martel did not exceed 1,000, but the statements both ways are unreliable. Only 80,000 fighting men, according to Saracen chronicles, were in the army, though the monks always claimed that several hundred thousand were north of the Pyrenees. Certain it is that the army was annihilated, the leader killed, and the plunder recaptured. Their own writers speak of their defeat as a most "disgraceful overthrow," and it is reasonable to suppose that Martel had accomplished his victory with an inferior force.

The Battle of Tours freed Gaul at once from further assault for a long time to come. It is true that the Saracens made one more effort to invade France by moving up the valley of the Rhone, but the attempt was speedily and sharply checked. The death of Charles left his sons, Carloman and Pepin, to divide the Frankish empire, but the latter soon assumed the title of king, became possessed of the whole of France, and, when he in turn died, in 768, the kingdom was again divided between two sons, Carloman and Charles; again, the elder speedily died, leaving undivided sovereignty to the younger brother.

When just twenty-eight years of age Charles, second son of Pepin, grandson of Charles Martel, became head of the whole empire of the west, and with wonderful skill, vigour and address extended its limits in every direction, building up a magnificent Christian empire that soon included Rome itself within its territory, and, in the year 800, he was solemnly crowned at St Peter's Emperor of the Roman Empire of the West, and became to history Charles the Great—Charlemagne.

The Franks from Clotaire III to Charles Martel

By Walter Copland Perry

At the death of Clotaire III. in Neustria (in *A.D.* 670), the whole empire was thrown into confusion by the ambitious projects of Ebroin, his *major-domus*, who sought to place Theoderic III., Clotaire's youngest brother, who was still a mere child, on the throne, that he might continue to reign in his name. Ebroin appears to have proceeded towards his object with too little regard for the opinions and feelings of the other *seigniors*, who rose against him and his puppet king, and drove them from the seat of power. The successful conspirators then offered the crown of Neustria to Childeric II., King of Austrasia, who immediately proceeded to take possession, while Ebroin sought refuge in a monastery.

Childeric ascended the Neustrian throne without opposition; but his attempts to control the *seigniors*, one of whom, named Badilo, he is said to have scourged, gave rise to a formidable conspiracy; and he was soon afterwards assassinated, together with hi queen and son at Chelles. Wulfoald escaped with difficulty, and returned to Austrasia. Another son of Childeric, Childebert III., was then raised upon the shield by the *seigniors*, while the royal party brought forward Theoderic III. from the monastery to which he had retired, and succeeded in making good his claim. The turbulent and unscrupulous but able Ebroin ventured once more to leave his place of refuge, and by a long series of the most treacherous murders, and by setting up a pretender—as Clovis, a son of Clotaire III he succeeded (in *A.D.* 673 or 674) in forcing himself upon Theoderic as Major-Domus of Neustria.

In the meantime, Dagobert II., whom Grimoald had sent as a child to Ireland, and who had subsequently found a faithful friend in the well-known St. Wilfrid, Bishop of York, was recalled and placed on the Austrasian throne. But the restored prince soon (in *A.D.* 678) fell a victim to the intrigues of Ebroin, and the Neustrian faction among the *seigniors*, who aimed at bringing the whole empire under their own arbitrary power. Nor does it seem at all improbable that the ability and audacity of Ebroin might have enabled them to carry out their designs, had not Austrasia possessed a leader fully equal to the emergency. Pepin, surnamed of Heristal from a castle belonging to his family in the neighbourhood of Liége, was the son of Ansegisus by Begga, the illustrious daughter of Pepin of Landen. This great man, who proved himself worthy of his grandsire and his mother, was at this time associated with Duke Martin in the government of Austrasia, which to *A.D.* 630 had been administered by Wulfoald. (Begga is spoken of in the highest terms by the annalists.)

Martin and Pepin summoned their followers to a to meet the expected attack of the Neustrians. In the first instance, however, the Austrasians were surprised by the activity of Ebroin, who fell upon them before they had completed their preparations, and totally defeated them in the neighbourhood of Lucofaus, (Loixi near Laon?). Martin fled to the town of Laon; and the artifices by which his enemies lured him from this retreat to his destruction are worthy of notice, as giving us a remarkable picture of the manners of the period in general, and of the sad state of the Church in particular. Ebroin, hearing that his intended victim had reached a place of safety, despatched Agilbert, Bishop of Paris, and Probus, Bishop of Rheims, to persuade Martin to repair to the Neustrian camp.

In order to dispel the apprehensions with which he listened to them, these holy men went through the not unusual ceremony of swearing upon a receptacle containing sacred relics, that he should suffer no injury by following their advice. The bishops, however, to save themselves from the guilt of perjury, had taken care that the vessels, which were covered, should be left empty. Martin, whom they omitted to inform of this important fact, was satisfied with their oaths, and accompanied them to Ecri, where he and his followers were immediately assassinated, without, as was thought, any detriment to the faith of the envoys!

Pepin, however, was neither to be cajoled nor frightened into submission, and soon found himself at the head of a powerful force, consisting in part of Neustrian exiles, whom the tyranny of Ebroin had ruined or offended. A collision seemed inevitable, when the position of affairs was suddenly changed by the death of Ebroin, who was assassinated in *A.D.* 681 by Hermenfried, a distinguished Neustrian Frank. Waratto followed him in the mayoralty of Neustria, and seemed inclined to live on friendly terms with Pepin; but Gislemar, his son, who headed the party most hostile to Pepin, succeeded in getting possession of the government for a time, and renewed the war against the Austrasians. Gislemar's death (in *A.D.* 684), which the annalists attribute to the Divine anger, (*A Deo percussus*), restored Waratto to his former power; and hostilities ceased for a time. When Waratto also died, about two years after his undutiful son, he was succeeded by Berchar, his son-in-law, whom the annalist pithily describes as "*statura parvus, intellectu modicus*," (of small stature, moderate intellect.)

The insolent disregard which this man showed to the feelings and wishes of the most powerful Neustrians, induced many of them to make common cause with Pepin, to whom they are said to have bound themselves by hostages. In *A.D.* 687 Pepin was strong enough to assume the offensive; and, yielding to the entreaties of the Neustrian refugees, he sent an embassy to Theoderic III. to demand the restoration of the exiles to their confiscated lands. The King of Neustria, prompted by Berchar, his *major-domus*, haughtily replied that he would come himself and fetch his runaway slaves. Pepin then prepared for war, with the unanimous consent of the Austrasian seigniors, whose wishes he scrupulously consulted.

Marching through the *Silva Carbonaria* (in Belgium), he entered the Neustrian territory, and took post at Testri on the River Somme. (Near St. Quentin.) Theoderic and Berchar also collected a large army and marched to meet the invaders. The two armies encamped in sight of each other near the village of Testri, on opposite sides of the little River Daumignon, the Neustrians on the southern and the Austrasians on the northern bank. Whether from policy or a higher motive, Pepin displayed great unwillingness, even then, to bring the matter to extremities; and, sending emissaries into the camp of Theoderic, he once more endeavoured to negotiate; demanding, amongst other things, that the property of which the churches had been "despoiled by wicked tyrants" should be restored to them. He promised that, if his conditions of peace were accepted and the effusion of kindred blood prevented, he would give the king a large amount of silver and gold.

The wise and humane reluctance of Pepin was naturally construed by Theoderic and his "little minded" mayor into fear, and distrust of his army, which was inferior to their own in numbers: a haughty answer was returned, and all negotiations broken off. Both sides then prepared for the morrow's battle. Pepin, having passed the night in forming his plans, crossed the river before daybreak and drew up his army to the east of Theoderic's position, that the rising sun might blind the enemy. The spies of Theoderic reported that the Austrasian camp was deserted, on which the Neustrians were led out to pursue the flying foe. The mistake of the scouts was soon made clear by the vigorous onset of Pepin; and after a fierce but brief combat the Neustrians were totally defeated, and Theoderic and Berchar fled from the field. (Pepin was even more remarkable for personal courage than for his generalship. *Paullus Diaconus*, vi. He relates that on one occasion he rushed on the camp of his enemies with only one follower, and cut their general and his attendants to pieces in his tent.) The latter was slain by his own followers: the king was taken prisoner, but his life was mercifully spared.

The Battle of Testri is notable in Frankish history as that in which the death-stroke was given to the Merovingian dynasty, by an ancestor of a far more glorious race of monarchs. The chronicler Erchambertus says:

> From this time forward, the kings began to have only the
> royal name, and not the royal dignity.

A very striking picture of the Rois Fainéans has been handed
down to us by Einhard, the friend and secretary of Charlemagne,
in his famous life of his royal master.

> The race of the Merovingians, from which the Franks
> were formerly accustomed to choose their kings, is gener-
> ally considered to have ended with Chilperic; who, at the
> command of the Roman Pontiff Stephen, was deposed,
> shorn of his locks, and sent into a monastery. But although
> the stock died out with him, it had long been entirely
> without life and vigour, and had no distinction beyond
> the empty title of king; for the authority and government
> were in the hands of the highest officers of the palace,
> who were called *majores-domus*, and had the entire admin-
> istration of affairs.
>
> Nothing was left to the king, except that, contenting him-
> self with the mere royal name, he was allowed to sit on
> the thrown with long hair and unshorn beard, to play the
> part of a ruler, to hear the ambassadors from whatever
> part they might come, and at their departure to commu-
> nicate to them the answers which he had been taught
> or even commanded to make, as if by his own authority.
> Besides the worthless title of king, and a scanty mainte-
> nance, which the *major-domus* meted out according to his
> pleasure, the king possessed only one farm, and that by no
> means a lucrative one, on which he had a dwelling-house
> and a few servants, just sufficient to supply his most urgent
> necessities.
>
> Wherever he had to go, he travelled in a carriage drawn by
> a yoke of oxen and driven by a cowherd in rustic fashion.
> It was thus that he went to the palace, to the public as-
> sembly of the people, which met every year for the good
> of the kingdom; after which he returned home. But the
> whole administration of the state, and everything which

had to be regulated or executed, either at home or abroad, was carried on by the mayors.

The whole power of the three kingdoms was thus suddenly thrown into the hands of Pepin, who showed in his subsequent career that he was equal to the far more difficult task of keeping, by his wisdom and moderation, what he had gained by the vigour of his intellect and his undaunted valour. He, too, was happily free from the little vanity which takes more delight in the pomp than in the realities of power, and, provided he possessed the substantial authority, was contented to leave the royal name to others. He must have felt himself strong enough to do what his uncle, Grimoald, had vainly attempted, and his grandson happily accomplished; but he saw that by grasping at the shadow he might lose the substance.

He was surrounded by proud and suspicious seigniors, whose jealousy would have been more excited by his taking the title, than by his exercising the powers of a king; and, strange though it may seem, the reverence for the ancient race, and the notion of their exclusive and inalienable rights, were far from being extinguished in the breasts of the common people. By keeping Theodoric upon the throne and ruling in his name, he united both reason and prejudice in support of his government. Yet some approach was made—though probably not by his own desire—towards acknowledged sovereignty in the case of Pepin. He was called *Dux et Princeps Francorum*, and the years of his office were reckoned, as well as those of the king, in all public documents.

Having fixed the seat of his government in Austrasia, as the more German and warlike portion of his dominions, he named dependents of his own, and subsequently his two sons, Drogo and Grimoald, to rule as mayors in the two other divisions of the empire. He gave the greatest proof of his power and popularity by restoring the assemblies of the Campus Martius, a purely German institution, which under the Romanising Merovingian monarchs had gradually declined. At these annual meetings, which were held on the 1st of March, the whole nation assembled for the purpose of discussing measures for the ensuing year. None but a ruler who was conscious of his own strength, and of an honest desire for the welfare of his people, would have voluntarily submitted himself and his actions to the chances of such an ordeal.

As soon as he had firmly fixed himself in his seat, and secured the submission of the envious seigniors, and the love of the people, who looked to him as the only man who could save them from the evils of anarchy, he turned his attention to the re-establishment of the Frankish empire in its full extent. The neighbouring tribes, which had with difficulty, and for the most part imperfectly, been subdued by Clovis and his successors, were ready to seize upon every favourable occasion of ridding themselves of the hated yoke.

Nor were the poor imbecile boys who bore the name of kings, or the turbulent mayors and seigniors, who were wholly occupied with plotting and counterplotting, railing and fighting, against one another, at all in a position to call the subject states to account, or to excite in them the desire of being incorporated with an empire harassed and torn by intestine dissensions. The Frankish empire was in process of dissolution, and all the more distant tribes, as the Bavarians, the Alemannians, Frisians, Bretons, and Gascons, had virtually recovered their independence. But this partial decline of the Frankish power was simply the result of misgovernment, and the domestic feuds which absorbed the martial vigour of the nation; and by no means indicated the decline of a military spirit in the Frankish people.

They only needed a centre of union and a leader worthy of them, both of which they found in Pepin, to give them once more the hegemony over all the German tribes, and prepare them for the conquest of Europe. The Frisians were subdued, or rather repressed for a time, in *A.D.* 697, after a gallant resistance under their king, Ratbod; and about twelve years afterwards we find the son of Pepin, Grimoald, forming a matrimonial alliance with Theudelinda, daughter of the Frisian monarch; a fact which plainly implies that Pepin desired to cultivate the friendship of his warlike neighbours. The Suabians, or Alemanni, were also attacked and defeated by Pepin on their own territories; but their final subjection was completed by his son Carl (Charles) Martel.

The wars carried on by Pepin with the above-mentioned nations, to which in this place we can only briefly allude, occupied him nearly twenty years; and were greatly instrumental in preserving peace at home, and consolidating the foundations of the Carlovingian throne. The stubborn resistance he met with from the still heathen Germans, was animated with something of that zeal, against which his great descendant Charlemagne had to contend in his interminable Saxon wars; for the adoption of Christianity, which was hated, not only as being hostile to the superstitions of their forefathers, but on account of the heavy taxes by which it was accompanied, was always made by Pepin the indispensable condition of mercy and peace.

But, happily for the cause of Gospel truth, other means were used for the spread of Christianity than the sword and the scourge; and the labours of many a zealous and self-sacrificing missionary from Ireland and England, served to convince the rude German tribes, that the warrior-priests whom they had met on the battlefield, and the greedy tax-gatherers who infested their homes, were not the true ambassadors of the Prince of Peace. And Pepin, who was by no means a mere warrior, was well aware of the value of these peaceful efforts; and afforded zealous aid to all who ventured their lives in the holy cause of human improvement and salvation. The civil governors whom he established in the conquered provinces were directed to do all in their power to promote the spread of Christianity by peaceful means; and, to give effect to his instructions, Pepin warned them that he should hold them responsible for the lives of his pious missionaries.

During these same twenty years, in which Pepin was playing the important and brilliant part assigned to him by Providence, the pale and bloodless shadows of four Merovingian kings flit gloomily across the scene. We know little or nothing of them except their names, and the order in which they followed each other. Theoderic III. died *A.D.* 691, and was succeeded by Clovis III., who reigned till *A.D.* 695 and was followed by Childebert III. On the death of Childebert in *A.D.* 711, Pepin raised

Dagobert III. to the nominal throne, where he left him when he himself departed from the scene of his labours and triumphs; and this is really all that we feel called upon to say of the descendants of the conquerors of Gaul and founders of the Western Empire; "*inclitum et notum olim, nunc tantum auditur!*) (Once a famous known, but now we only hear!)

The extraordinary power which Pepin exercised at a period when law was weak, and authority extended no further than the sword could reach; when the struggles of the rising feudal aristocracy for independence had convulsed the empire and brought it to the verge of anarchy, sufficiently attests the ability and courage, the wisdom and moderation, with which he ruled. His triumphs over the ancient dynasty, and the Neustrian faction, were far from being the most difficult of his achievements. He had to control' the very class to which he himself belonged; to curb the turbulent spirits of the very men who had raised him to his proud pre-eminence; and to establish regal authority over those by whose aid he had humbled the ancient kings: and all this he succeeded in doing by the extraordinary influence of his personal character. So firmly indeed had he established his government, and subdued the wills of the envious *seigniors* by whom he was surrounded, that even when he allowed his intention of making his power hereditary in his family, they dared not, at the time, oppose his will. (Fredeg. *Chron. Cont.*)

On the death of Norbert, *major-domus* at the court of Childebert III., Pepin—in all probability without even consulting the *seigniors*, in whom the right of election rested—appointed his second son Grimoald to the vacant office. To his eldest son Drogo, he had already given the Mayoralty of Burgundy, with the title of Duke of Campania. But though they dared not make any opposition at the time, it is evident from what followed that the fear of Pepin alone restrained the rage they felt at this open usurpation. In *A.D.* 714, when Pepin's life was drawing to a close, and he lay at Jopil near Liege upon a bed of sickness, awaiting patiently his approaching end, the great vassals took heart, and conspired to deprive his descendants of the mayoralty. They employed the usual means for effecting their purpose—

treachery and murder. (*Annal Mett.*).

Grimoald was assassinated, while praying in the Church of St. Lambert at Jopil, by a Frisian of the name of Rantgar, who relied, no doubt, on the complicity of the *seigniors* and the weakness of Pepin for impunity. But the conspirators had miscalculated the waning sands of the old warrior's life, and little knew the effect which the sight of his son's blood would have upon him. He suddenly recovered from the sickness to which he seemed to be succumbing. Like another Priam, he once more seized his unaccustomed arms, though, unlike the royal Trojan, he used them with terrible effect.

After taking an ample revenge upon the murderers of his son, and quenching the spirit of resistance in the blood of the conspirators, he was so far from giving up his purpose, or manifesting any consciousness of weakness, that he nominated the infant and illegitimate son of Grimoald, as if by hereditary right, to the joint mayoralty of Burgundy and Neustria—an office which the highest persons in the land would have been proud to exercise. By his very last act, therefore, he showed the absolute mastery he had obtained, not only over the "do-nothing" kings, but over the factious *seigniors*, who shrank in terror before the wrath of one who had, as it were, repassed the gates of death, to hurl destruction on their heads. His actual demise took place in the same year, on the 16th of December, *A.D.* 714.

Pepin had two wives, the first of whom, Plectrudis, bore him two sons, Drogo and Grimoald, neither of whom survived their father. In *A.D.* 688 he married a second wife, the "noble and elegant" Alpais, though Plectrudis was still alive. (Fred. *Chron. Cont.*) From this second marriage sprang the real successor of the Pepins, whom his father named in his own language Carl, and who is renowned in history as Carl Martel, the bulwark of Christendom, the father of kings and emperors.

Our estimate of the personal greatness of the Carlovingian mayors is greatly raised when we observe that each of them in turn, instead of taking quiet possession of what his predecessors had won, has to reconquer his position in the face of numerous, powerful and exasperated enemies. It was so with Pepin of

Landen, with Pepin of Heristal, and most of all in the case of Carl Martel.

At the death of Pepin, the storm which had long been gathering, and of which many forebodings had appeared in his lifetime, broke forth with tremendous fury. The bands of government were suddenly loosened, and the powers which Pepin had wielded with such strength and dexterity became the objects of a ferocious struggle. Plectrudis, his first wife, an ambitious and daring woman, had resolved to reign as the guardian of her grandchild, Theudoald, with whom she was at that time residing at Cologne. Theudoald had at least the advantage of being the only candidate for power installed by Pepin himself, and it was no doubt upon his quasi-hereditary claims that Plectrudis based her hopes.

She manifested her foresight, discrimination, and energy, at the commencement of the contest which ensued by seizing the person of Carl, her stepson, and most formidable rival. (*Annal Mett.*) But Carl and his party were not her only opponents. The Neustrians and Burgundians, whom their recollections of Brunhilda and Fredegunda by no means inclined to acquiesce in another female regency, refused obedience to her commands; and endeavoured to excite the puppet-monarch Dagobert to an independent exercise of his authority.

Their zeal as Neustrians too was quickened by the desire of throwing off the Austrasian or German yoke, which they considered to have been fixed upon them by the victories and energetic rule of Pepin. It was owing to this hostile feeling between the Romance and the German portions of the empire that many even of Pepin's partisans took side with Theudoald and Plectrudis, although the latter held their chief incarcerated. (The author of the *Annal. Mett* an. 715, charges them with ungratefully forgetting all the benefits conferred on them by Pepin.)

The revolted Neustrians and the army of Plectrudis encountered each other in the forest of Guise, near Compiegne; and, as far as one can conjecture from the confused and contradictory accounts of the annalists, Plectrudis and Theudoald suffered a defeat. The Neustrians having obtained the mastery over the hated Germans in their own country, prepared to extend their authority to Austrasia itself. Having chosen Raginfried as their *major-domus*, they suddenly marched into the Austrasian territory, and laid it waste with fire and sword as far as the River Meuse. In spite of their Christian profession they sought further to strengthen themselves by an alliance with Ratbod, the heathen King of the Frisians, who at the death of Pepin had recovered his independence, and the greater portion of his territory. (We gather this from the flight of Theudoald, *Fredeg . Chron. Cont.*)

In the meantime, the whole aspect of affairs was suddenly changed by the escape of Carl from custody. The defeated army of Plectrudis, and many of the Austrasian seigniors, who were unwilling to support her cause even against the Neustrians, now rallied with the greatest alacrity round the youthful hero, and proclaimed him *Dux Francorum* by the title of his glorious father. In a very short time after the recovery of his freedom, Carl found himself at the head of a very efficient, though not numerous army. He was still, however, surrounded by dangers and difficulties, under which a man of less extraordinary powers must inevitably have sunk.

Dagobert III. died soon after the Battle of Compiegne; and the Neustrians, who had felt the disadvantage of his imbecility, neglected the claims of his son, and raised a priest called Daniel, a reputed son of Childeric, to the throne, with the title of Chilperic II. (Fred. *Chron. Cont.*) This monarch, who appears to have had a greater degree of energy than his immediate predecessors, formed a plan with the Frisian king for a combined attack upon Cologne, by which he hoped at once to bring the war to a successful issue. Ratbod, true to his engagements, advanced with a numerous fleet of vessels up the Rhine, while Chilperic and Raginfried were marching towards Cologne through the forest of Ardennes. To prevent this well-planned junction, Carl determined to fall upon the Frisians before they reached Cologne. His position must have been rendered still more critical by the failure of this attack. We read that after both parties had suffered considerable loss in a hard-fought battle, they retreated on equal terms. (*Annal. Met.*)

The short time which elapsed before the arrival of the Neustrians was spent by Carl in summoning his friends from every quarter, to assist him in the desperate struggle in which he was engaged. In the meantime, Chilperic came up, and, encamping in the neighbourhood of Cologne, effected a junction with the Franks. Contrary to expectation, however, no attack was made upon Plectrudis, who is said to have bribed the Frisians to retire. A better reason for the precipitate retreat of the Neustrians and Frisians (which now took place) was the danger which the former ran of having their retreat cut off by Carl, who had taken up a strong position in their rear, with continually increasing forces; as it was, they were not permitted to retire in safety. Carl attacked them at Ambleve, near Stablo, in the Ardennes, and gave them a total defeat. This victory put him in possession of Cologne, and the person of Plectrudis, who restored to him his father's treasures.

In the following year, *A.D.* 717, Carl assumed the offensive, and, marching through the *Silva Carbonaria*, began to lay waste the Neustrian territory, Chilperic and Raginfried advanced to meet him, doubtless with far less confidence than before; and both armies encamped at Vinci, in the territory of Cambrai. Carl, with an hereditary moderation peculiarly admirable in a man of his warlike spirit, sent envoys to the Neustrian camp to offer conditions of peace; and to induce Chilperic to acknowledge his claim to the office of *major-domus* in Austrasia, "that the blood of so many noble Franks might not be shed." (*Annal. Mett.*) Carl himself can have expected no other fruit from these overtures than the convincing of his own followers of the unreasonableness of their enemies.

The Neustrian king and his evil adviser rejected the preferred terms with indignation, and declared their intention of taking from Carl even that portion of his inheritance which had already fallen into his hands. Both sides then prepared for battle; Carl, as we are expressly told, having first communicated to the chief men in his camp the haughty and threatening answer of the king. Chilperic relied on his great superiority in numbers, though his army was drawn, for the most part, from the dregs of the people: Carl prepared to meet him with a small but highly-disciplined force of well-armed and skilful warriors. In the battle which ensued on the 21st of March, the Neustrians were routed with tremendous loss, and pursued by the victors to the very gates of Paris. But Carl was not yet in a condition to keep possession of Neustria, and he therefore led his army back to Cologne, and ascended the "throne of his kingdom," as the annalist already calls it, the *dignissimus haeres* (worthy heir), of his mighty father.

The unfortunate Chilperic, unequal as he must have felt himself to cope with a warrior like Carl, was once more induced by evil counsellors to renew the war. With this view he sought the alliance of the imperfectly subjected neighbouring states, whom the death of Pepin had awakened to dreams of independence. Of these the foremost was Aquitaine, which had completely emancipated itself from Frankish rule. The Aquitania of the Roman Empire extended, as is well known, from the Pyrenees to the River Loire.

This country, at the dissolution of the Western Empire, had fallen into the hands of the Visigoths, and was subsequently conquered, and to a certain extent subjugated, by the earlier Merovingians. But, though nominally part of the Frankish empire, it continued to enjoy a semi-independence under its native dukes, and remained for many ages a stone of offence to the Frankish rulers. Its population, notwithstanding the admixture of German blood consequent on the Gothic conquest, had remained pre-eminently Roman in its character, and had attained in the seventh century to an unusual degree of wealth and civilisation. The southern part of Aquitaine had been occupied by a people called Vascones or Gascons, who extended themselves as far as the Garonne, and had also submitted to the Frankish rule during the better days of the elder dynasty.

The temporary collapse of the Frankish power consequent upon the bloody feuds of the royal house, and the struggle between the *seigniors* and the crown, enabled Eudo, the Duke of Aquitaine, to establish himself as a perfectly independent Prince;

and he and his sons ruled in full sovereignty over both Aquitaine and Gascony, and were called indifferently *Aquitaniae* or *Vasconiae duces*, (leaders).

Under these circumstances, it is not to be wondered at that Eudo should gladly receive the presents and overtures made to him by Chilperic; who agreed to leave him in quiet possession of the independence he had contumaciously asserted, on condition of his making cause against the Austrasian mayor. He lost no time in leading an army of Gascons to Paris, where he joined his forces to those of Chilperic, and prepared to meet the terrible foe. Carl advanced with his usual rapidity, and having laid waste a portion of Neustria, came upon the enemy in the neighbourhood of Soissons. The new allies, who had scarcely had time to consolidate their union and mature their plans, appear to have made but a feeble resistance; and Chilperic, not considering himself safe even in Paris, fled with his treasures, in company with Eudo, into Aquitaine. Raginfried, the Neustrian *major-domus*, who with a division of the combined army had also made an attempt to check Carl's progress, was likewise defeated and compelled to resign his mayoralty; as a compensation for which he received from the placable conqueror the countship of Anjou.

The victorious Austrasians pursued the fugitives, as far as the river Loire and Orleans, from which place Carl sent an embassy to Eudo, and offered him terms of peace, on condition of his delivering up Chilperic and his treasures. It is difficult to say what answer Eudo, hemmed in as he was on all sides (for the Saracens were in his rear), might have given to this demand,—whether he would have consulted his own interests, or his duty to his ally and guest. But the opportune death of Clotaire, whom Carl had made king of Austrasia after the Battle of Ambleve, relieved him from his dilemma.

Carl, who was remarkably free from the evil spirit of revenge, declared his readiness to acknowledge Chilperic II. as king, on condition of being himself appointed *major-domus* of the united kingdoms of Austrasia, Neustria, and Burgundy. These terms, offered by the victor to one whose very life was at his mercy, could not but be eagerly accepted; and thus, in *A.D.* 719, Carl became nominally Mayor of the Palace to King Chilperic II., but, in fact, undisputed master of the king himself and the whole Frankish empire.

The temperate course pursued by Carl in these transactions, proceeded in a great measure from the natural moderation of his character; but it was a course which the coolest calculation would suggest. He was indeed victorious, but he was still surrounded by enemies who were rather beaten than subdued, and many of them were those of his own household.

After the death of Ratbod, the "cruel and pagan" King of the Frisians, in *A.D.* 719, Carl recovered the western portion of Friesland, and reduced the Frisians to their former state of uncertain subjection. (*Annal. Mett.*) About the same time, he repelled the Saxons, those unwearied and implacable enemies of the Frankish name, who had broken into the Frankish *gaus* on the right bank of the Rhine. We know little of the particulars of these campaigns, since the chroniclers content themselves with recording in general terms that the "invincible Carl" was always victorious, and his enemies utterly destroyed; a statement which is rendered suspicious by the fact that their annihilation has to be repeated frequently, and at no long intervals.

In the year after the Saxon campaign (the date of which is rather uncertain), Carl crossed the Rhine, and attacked the Alemanni (in Wirtemberg) in their own country, which he devastated without any serious opposition. Subsequently, about *A.D.* 725, he crossed the Danube, and entered the country of the Bavarians; and after two successful campaigns obliged that nation also to acknowledge their allegiance to the Franks. The chronicler says:

> "From this expedition, he returned by the Lord's assistance to his own dominions with great treasures and a certain matron, by name Plectrude, and her niece Sonihilde." (*Annal. Mett.*) This latter, who is called by Einhard "Swanahilde, the niece of Odilo," subsequently became one of Carl's wives, and the mother of the unfortunate Gripho.

It seems natural to conjecture, that Carl had an important ulterior object before his mind in these extraordinary and sustained exertions. They were but the prelude to the grand spectacle soon to be presented to an admiring world, in which this mighty monarch with the humble name was to play a conspicuous and glorious part. A contest awaited him, which he must long have foreseen with mingled feelings of eagerness and apprehension, and into which he dared not go unprepared; a contest which required the highest exercise of his own active genius, and the uncontrolled disposal of all the material resources of his empire.

He had hitherto contended for his hereditary honours against his personal enemies—for the supremacy of the Germans over the Gallo Romans, of his own tribe over kindred German tribes—and finally, for order and good government against anarchy and faction. Hereafter he was to renew the old struggle between the West and East—to be the champion of Christianity and German Institutions, against the faith of Mohammed.

The successors of the prophet had conquered and converted, not Arabia alone, but Syria, Persia, Palestine, Phoenicia, Egypt, Asia Minor, Armenia, the country between the Black Sea and the Caspian, a portion of India, and the whole of the North of Africa from the Nile to the Atlantic Ocean.

The year *A.D.* 710 found them gazing with longing eyes across the straits of Gibraltar, eager for the time when they might plant upon the rock of Calpe the meteor standard of their prophet; and thence survey the beautiful and fertile country which was soon to be their own. Nor were their hopes deferred; their entrance into Spain, which might have proved difficult if not impossible to effect in the face of a brave and united people, was rendered safe and easy by treachery, cowardice, and theological dissensions.

The first collision, indeed, of the Arabian conquerors with the warriors of the West was rather calculated to damp their hopes of European conquest. The Visigothic kings of Spain possessed the town of Ceuta on the African coast, of which Count Julian, at the time of which we speak, was military governor.

The skill and courage of this great warrior and his garrison, had hitherto frustrated all the attempts of Musa, the general of the Caliph Walid, to make himself master of the place. The Saracens were already beginning to despair of success, when they suddenly received overtures from Count Julian himself, who now offered, not merely to open the gate of Ceuta, but to procure for the Saracens a ready admittance into Spain. The grounds of this sudden treachery on the part of one who had risked his life at the post of honour, cannot be stated with any degree of certainty.

By some it was ascribed to the desire of avenging himself upon Roderic, his king, who is said to have abused his daughter; and by others to the fact that he had espoused the cause of Witiza's sons, at that time pretenders to the Spanish throne. The Saracen general, Musa, delighted to found the Achilles-heel of Europe, immediately despatched a few hundred Moslems across the strait, under the command of Tarik; from whom the modern Gibraltar (Gebel-al-Tarik) derives its name. These adventurers were well received in the town and castle of Count Julian at Algesiras, and soon returned to expectant comrades, with rich booty and exciting tales of the fertility of the country, and the degenerate Goths.

In the April of the following year, *A.D.* 711, a body of 5000 Saracens effected a landing on the coast of Spain, and entrenched themselves strongly near the Rock of Gibraltar. These were soon followed by other troops, until a considerable Moslem Army was collected on the Spanish shores. The feeble resistance made to this descent was a fatal omen for the empire of the Visigoths. This once brave and hardy tribe of Germans had lost, during a long peace, the valour and endurance to which they owed the rich provinces of Spain; and, amidst the pleasures of that luxurious country, had grown so unaccustomed to the use of arms, that it was long before they could be roused to meet the foe.

At length, however, the unwarlike Roderic, having collected an army four times as great as that of the enemy, but without confidence either in their leader or themselves, encamped at Xeres de la Frontera, in the neighbourhood of Cadiz. (*Chron*

Moissiac.) While awaiting at this place the approach of the enemy, the Gothic king is represented as sitting in an ivory chariot, arrayed in silken garments unworthy of a man even in time of peace, and wearing a golden crown upon his head. The battle which quickly followed was fought on the 26th of July, *A.D.* 731. It was of short duration and of no doubtful issue. The timid herd of Goths, scarcely awaiting the wild charge of the Saracens, turned and fled in irretrievable confusion. Roderic himself, fit leader of such an army, was among the first to leave the field on the back of a fleet racer, which had been placed, at his desire, in the neighbourhood of his tent, as if his trembling heart had foreseen the issue.

The Visigothic Empire in Spain fell by a single blow. Tarik advanced with his victorious army as far as Cordova, which immediately yielded at his summons; and he would, without doubt, have overrun the whole of Spain, had he not been recalled by the jealousy of Musa, who reserved for himself the glory of completing the splendid conquest.

Of all the Spanish towns which were captured on occasion, Seville and Merida alone appear to have upheld the ancient glories of the Gothic name; but even these were finally reduced, and the last remnants of the Visigoths were driven from the rich plains they had so long possessed into the mountains of Asturias. It was in these rugged solitudes, and amidst the hardships and privations which they there endured, that they regained their ancient vigour, and preserved their Christian faith. It was thence that at a later period they descended upon their Moorish foes, and in many a hard-fought battle, the frequent theme of ballad and romaunt, recovered, step by step, the fair possessions which their ancestors had won and lost.

And thus, by a single victory Spain was added to the vast dominions of the Caliph, and the Cross once more retired before the Crescent. Nor did it seem that the Pyrenees, any more than the rock of Gibraltar, were to prove a barrier to the devastating flood of Islamism. About *A.D.* 718, Zama, the Arabian Viceroy of Spain, made himself master of that portion of Gaul, on the slopes of the Eastern Pyrenees, of which the Goths had hith-

MUSLIM TROOPS LEAVING NARBONNE

erto retained possession. In *A.D.* 731 he stormed Narbonne, the capital of the province, and having put all the male inhabitants capable of bearing arms to the sword, he sent away the women and children into captivity.

He then pushed forward into Aquitaine, and laid siege to Toulouse, which proved the limit of his progress; for it was there that he was defeated by Eudo, the duke of the country, who was roused to a desperate effort by the danger of his capital. (Roderic. *Hist. Arab.*) The check thus given to the onward march of the Moslems was of short duration. Ambiza, the successor of Zama, about four years afterwards once more made a movement in advance. Taking a more easterly direction, he stormed and plundered Carcassonne and Nismes; and having devastated the country as far as the Rhone, returned laden with booty across the Pyrenees. (*Chron. Moissiac.*)

Duke Eudo of Aquitaine, deprived of the fruits of his single victory, resigned all hopes of successfully resisting the invaders, and endeavoured to preserve himself from utter ruin by an alliance with his formidable foes. He is even said to have so far belied his character of Christian prince as to give his own daughter in marriage, or concubinage, to Munuz, the governor of the newly-made Gallic conquests. (Marca de Marc. *Hispan.* ii.)

It appears that the expeditions of the Saracens into Gaul had been hitherto made by individual generals on a comparatively small scale, and on their own responsibility. The unusually slow progress of their arms at this period, is to be ascribed less to any fear of opposition, than to inward dissensions in the Arabian empire, and a rapid succession of *caliphs* singularly unlike in their characters and views. Nine short years (*A.D.* 715—724,) had seen the cruel Soliman succeeded by the severe, yet just and upright Omar, the luxurious Epicurean Yesid, and the little-minded, calculating Hescham.

It is probable, therefore, that, amid more pressing anxieties and interests, the distant conquest of Spain was forgotten or neglected by the court at Damascus; and that the generals, who commanded in that country, were apt to indulge in ideas inconsistent with their real position as satraps and slaves of an imperial master. But a change was at hand, and the new actor Abder-rahman, who suddenly appeared upon the scene with an army of 400,000 men, was charged with a twofold commission,—to chastise the presumption of Munuz, whose alliance with Eudo was regarded with suspicion,—and to bring the whole of Gaul under the sceptre of the *caliph* and the law of Mohammed.

Regarding Munuz as a rebel and a semi-apostate, Abderrah-man besieged him in the town of Cerdagne, to which he fled for refuge, and, having driven him to commit suicide, sent his head, together with his wife, the daughter of Eudo, as a welcome present to the Caliph Hescham.

★★★★★★

(Roderic *Hist Arab*. c. 13. Ex *Chron. Isidori*, an. 731 Munuz meets with no pity from the Episcopal Chronicler. His fate befell him, "*judicio Deo*," (God's judgement), because he was "drunk with the blood of Christians," and was al-ready "*satis damnatus ab hoc*" (sentenced by), that had burnt Bishop Anambadus.

★★★★★★

The victorious Saracens then marched on past Pampeluna, and, making their way through the narrow defiles on the west-ern side of the Pyrenean chain, poured down upon the plains with their innumerable hosts as far as the River Garonne. The city of Bordeaux was taken and sacked, and still they pressed on impetuously and without opposition, until they reached the River Dordogne, where Eudo, burning with rage at the treat-ment which his daughter had received, made a fruitless attempt to stop them. Irritated rather than checked by his feeble efforts, the overwhelming tide poured on. The standard of the Prophet soon floated from the towers of Poitiers, and even Tours, the city of the holy St. Martin, was in danger when, in the hour of Eu-rope's greatest dread and danger, the champion of Christendom appeared at last, to do battle with hitherto triumphant enemies.

It seems strange at first sight that the danger, which had so long been threatening Europe from the side of Spain, should not have called forth an earlier and more effectual resistance from those whose national and religious existence was at stake.

Abderrahman had now made his way into the very centre of modern France; had taken and plundered some of the wealthiest towns in the Frankish empire; and, after burning or desecrating every Christian church he met with, was marching on the hallowed sanctuary of the patron saint, enriched by the offerings of ages; without encountering a single foe who could even hope to stay his progress.

Where was the "invincible" and ubiquitous Carl, who was wont to fall like a thunderbolt upon his enemies? We might indeed be surprised at his seeming tardiness, did we not know the extraordinary difficulties with which he had to struggle, and the seemingly impossible task he had to perform. It was not with the Saracens alone, but with his barbarous kinsmen—with nations as hardy and warlike as his own Austrasian warriors, and animated no less than the followers of Mohammed with an indomitable hatred of the Christian name. Enemies were ready to pour upon him from every side, from the green slopes of the Pyrenees and over the broad waters of the Rhine; nor could he reckon upon the fidelity of all who lay within these boundaries.

During the whole of the ten years in which the Saracens were crossing the Pyrenees and establishing themselves in Gaul, Carl was constantly engaged in wars with his German neighbours. In that short period, he made campaigns against the Frisians, the Swabians, and the Bavarians, the last of whom (as we have seen) he even crossed the Danube to attack in their own country. As late as *A.D.* 728, when Abderrahman must have been already meditating his desolating march, Carl had to turn his arms once more against the Saxons; and in *A.D.* 731, the very year before he met the Saracens at Poitiers, he marched an army into Aquitaine to quell the rebellion of Duke Eudo.

Such were some of the adverse circumstances under which Carl had to make his preparations, and under which he encamped with his veterans in the neighbourhood of Poitiers, where, for the first time in his life, he beheld the white tents of the Moslem invaders, covering the land as far as the eye could reach.

We cannot doubt that he had long been looking forward

to this hour with an anxious though intrepid heart, for all depended upon him; and that the wars in which he had lately been engaged, were the more important in his eyes, because their successful termination was necessary to secure his rear, and increase the limits of his warband when the time for action, should arrive.

The hitherto unconquered Saracens, who had carried the banner of their Prophet in almost uninterrupted triumph from the deserts of Arabia to the banks of the Loire, were destined to find at last an insuperable barrier in Carl and his Austrasian followers.

On a Sunday, in the month of October, *A.D.*732, after trying each other's strength in skirmishes of small importance during the whole of the previous week, the two armies, invoking respectively the aid of Christ and Mohammed, came to a general engagement on the plains between Poitiers and Tours. The rapid onslaught of the Ishmaelites, by which they were accustomed to bear everything before them, recoiled from the steady front of the Franks, whose heavy swords made dreadful havoc among their lightly clad opponents.

Repulsed, but unbroken in courage and determination, resolved to force their way through that wall of steel or to dash themselves to death against it, the gallant Moslems repeated their wild charges until sunset. At every repulse their blood flowed in torrents, and at the end of the day they found themselves farther than from the goal, and gazed upon far more dead upon the slippery field than remained alive in their ranks. Hopeless of being able to renew the contest, they retreated in the night, and, for the first time, fled before an enemy.

On the following morning, when the Franks again drew up in battle-array, the camp of the foe was discovered to be empty, so that, instead of awaiting the attack, they had the more agreeable task of plundering the tents and pursuing the fugitives. Abderrahman himself was found among the dead, and around him, according to the not very credible account of the chroniclers, lay 300,000 of his soldiers; while the Franks lost only 500 men. (*Reginon Chron.*; Paull. Diacon. vi. 46. says that the Saracens lost

THE BATTLE OF POITIERS

375,000!)

Eudo, who, after his defeat on the Dordogne, had taken refuge with his more merciful enemy Carl, was present in the battle and took part in the pursuit and plunder. It was after this glorious triumph over the most formidable enemies of his country and religion that Carl received the surname of Martel (the hammer), by which he has since been known in history.

The importance of this victory to all succeeding ages has often been enlarged upon, and can hardly be exaggerated. The fate of Europe, humanly speaking, hung upon the sword of the Frankish mayor; and but for Carl, and the bold German warriors who had learned the art and practice of war under him and his glorious father, the heart of Europe might have been in the possession of the Moslems.

Though an effective check had been given to the progress of the Saracen arms, and they themselves had been deprived of that chief support of valour,—the belief in their own invincibility,—yet their power was by no means broken, nor was Carl in a condition to improve his victory. The Neustrians and Burgundians were far from being reconciled to the supremacy which the German Franks had acquired over themselves under the mighty Carlovingian mayors.

Their jealousy of Carl Martel's success and their hatred of his person, were so much stronger than their zeal in the cause of Christendom, that even while he was engaged in his desperate conflict with the Saracens, they were raising a rebellion in his rear. But the indefatigable warrior was not sleeping on the fresh laurels he had won. No sooner had he received intelligence of their treacherous designs, than he led his troops, fresh from the slaughter of the *infidels*, into the very heart of Burgundy, and inflicted a terrible retribution on his domestic foes. He then removed all whom he had reason to suspect from their posts of emolument and honour, and bestowed them upon men on whom he could depend in the hour of danger.

In the following year, *A. D.* 734, he made considerable progress in the subjugation and, what was even more difficult, the conversion of the Frisians, who hated Christianity the more be-

The Battle of Poitiers

cause it was connected in their minds with a foreign yoke. The preaching of Boniface was powerfully seconded by the sword of Carl, who attacked them by land and sea, defeated their Duke, Poppo, destroyed their heathen altars, and, like our own Alfred in the case of the Danes, gave them the alternative of Christianity or death.

After the victory of Poitiers, Carl had entrusted the defence of the Pyrenean borders to Duke Eudo, whom he left in peaceable though dependent possession of his territories. Eudo had received a rough lesson from his former misfortunes, and passed the remainder of his life in friendly relations with his Frankish liege lord. At the death of Eudo, in *A.D.* 735, a dispute arose between his sons, Hunold and Hatto, respecting the succession; and it seems that in the course of their contest they had forgotten their common dependence upon Carl Martel. A feud of this nature at such a period, and in the immediate neighbourhood of the Saracens, was highly dangerous to Aquitaine and the whole Frankish empire.

Carl therefore lost no time in leading an army into the distracted province, to settle the disputes of the contending parties, and bring the population into a more complete state of subjection. Having advanced to the Garonne and taken the city of Bordeaux, he entered into negotiations with Hunold; and, "with his accustomed piety," conferred the duchy upon him, on condition of his renewing his father's oath of fealty to himself and his two sons, whom he thus distinctly pointed out to the Franks as their hereditary rulers. (*Annal Mett.*)

In *A. D.* 737, the Moslems were once more introduced into the south of Gaul by the treachery of Christians. A man of influence in Provence, called Maurontus, who probably aimed at an independent dukedom, formed a strong party among the Neustrian *seigniors* against the detested German mayor. As the Arabian alliance was the only one which could sustain them in a conflict with Carl, they made no scruple of inviting Ibn Jussuf, the new viceroy of Septimania (Languedoc), into their country and giving him the city of Avignon as a pledge of their sincerity. The Saracens, instructed by their strange allies, passed into

Burgundy, where the party opposed to Carl was strongest: having taken Vienne, they covered the country as far as Lyons with their wild and rapid cavalry, which everywhere left its traces of fire and blood.

The advance of the Saracens was so sudden, and their progress so rapid, that Carl Martel was not immediately prepared to meet them. He therefore despatched his brother Childebrand and his principal *seigniors*, with such forces as were ready, to keep the enemy in check; determining himself to follow with a numerous and well appointed army. When the advanced guard of the Franks arrived near Avignon, the Saracens retreated into that place, and prepared to stand a siege. On the arrival of Carl, the town, which had resisted Childebrand, was taken by storm, and the Arabian garrison put to the sword.

The Franks then crossed the Rhone, and marched through Septimania to Narbonne—a place of great importance to the Saracens, who had made it a magazine for their arms. It was defended at this time by Athima, viceroy of the *Caliph* in Septimania, with a considerable force. The Saracens of Spain, fearing that the garrison might be insufficient to withstand the assault of the Franks (who had invested the town on every side), fitted out a fleet, and transported a body of troops to the mouth of the River Berre (near Narbonne), in hopes of raising the siege.

This movement did not escape the quick eye of Carl; who, leaving his brother with a division of the besiegers, fell with the remainder on the newly landed force of the enemy, and routed them with dreadful slaughter. He failed, however, in his attempts upon Narbonne, which remained in the hands of the Saracens; while Bezières, Agde, Megalone, and Nismes, together with all the territory on the north side of the River Aude (subsequently known as Languedoc), were reunited to the Frankish Empire.

According to Paullus Diaconus, Carl Martel was assisted on this occasion by Luitprand, King of the Langobards in Italy, with whom he had formed a close alliance and friendship. (Paull. Diac. *Gest. Longob.* Carl sent his son Pepin to Luitprand at Pavia; that the Lombard king, "*juxta morem*," might cut off his first hair,—an especial mark of friendship and honour.) We have hardly sufficient grounds for believing; that the Langobards took an active part in this war, but the mere expectation of their approach may have exercised some influence in bringing about the results above described.

The activity of his enemies in the north again prevented Carl from pursuing his advantages against the Moslems, who might perhaps, had German Europe been united, have even then been driven back to the shores of Africa. In *A. D.* 737 we find the indefatigable warrior employed in repelling and avenging a fresh inroad of the Saxons, whom he defeated with great slaughter and drove along the river Lippe. In *A. D.* 739 he again appeared in Burgundy, where his presence had become necessary to stamp out the smouldering embers of the old conspiracy.

In the meantime, a new theatre was preparing for the Franks, on which they were destined by Providence to play a very conspicuous and important part. The exertions and influence of Boniface the great apostle of Germany, and the intimate religious union he had effected between the Frankish Church and the Bishops of Rome, were to produce for both parties still richer fruits than had yet appeared. To understand the circumstances which brought them into closer external relations, corresponding to the increased intimacy of their spiritual union, it will be necessary to make ourselves acquainted with the state of Italy at this period; and more especially with the very singular and anomalous position of the Bishops of Rome.

That devoted land, as if in penance for the long and selfish tyranny it had exercised over the world, had become the prey, in turn, of almost every barbarous tribe of Europe; but was at this period nominally subject to the Emperors of the East. The victories of Narses, in *A. D.* 534, had destroyed the power of the Ostrogoths, which, under the great and good Theoderic, had seemed so firmly established; and Italy was now a province of the Roman Empire, instead of being, as formerly, its centre and head. It was governed for the Byzantine court by a viceroy styled Exarch, whose residence was at Ravenna, on the eastern coast. The court and people of Constantinople, however, were too feeble to retain for any length of time a conquest, which they owed solely to the genius of a fortunate general. About thirty years after the defeat of the Goths, when the valiant eunuch had ceased to defend what he had won, the Langobards and 20,000 Saxons, descending upon Italy from the Julian Alps, expelled the Romans from the greater portion of their recent conquests, and confined them to the narrow limits of the Exarchate.

The empire which the Langobards at this time established was greatly weakened by its division into several Duchies, the rulers of which were in constant strife with one another and with the central government. We may judge of the extent and consequences of these internal dissensions from the fact that, after the assassination of King Kleph (*A.D.* 574), the Langobards in Italy remained without a king for ten years, and were subject to thirty-six dukes, each of whom "reigned in his own city." The most powerful of these were the Dukes of Benevento, Friuli, and Spoleto. (Paull. Diacon.)

At the end of this period the royalist party—favoured, no doubt, by the great mass of the people, to whom nothing is so hateful as a petty tyrant—once more obtained the ascendancy, and compelled the revolted dukes to swear fealty to Authari, surnamed Flavius, son of the murdered Kleph. The reunion of the Langobards under one head was naturally followed by a further extension of their borders at the expense of the Roman empire; and this extension was the immediate cause of a collision between the kings of the Langobards and the successors of St. Peter, which gave rise to the most important and lasting results.

The Bishops of Rome had, in the meantime, been adding to the spiritual influence they owed to their position as heads of the Church in the great capital of the West, the material resources of extensive possessions, and numerous and devoted vassals. Like all other dignified ecclesiastics within the imperial dominions, the Bishops of Rome were subject to the Greek Emperor; but, as it was mainly by their influence and exertions that the city and duchy of Rome were kept in allegiance to the Greek Emperor, the balance of obligation was generally in favour of the *Pontiffs*, who, on that account, were treated by the court at

Constantinople in a far less arrogant manner than would have been congenial to the pompous sovereigns of the East.

The aggressive attitude of the Langobards, which threatened the Greek Emperors with the loss of the small remnant of their Italian possessions, was calculated to excite no less the apprehensions of the Roman Bishops. It was open to them, indeed, to throw themselves at once into the arms of the Langobardian monarchs, from whose reverence and gratitude they might, no doubt, have acquired a commanding position in Church and State; and it was this ever-present alternative which rendered them virtually independent of their nominal sovereigns.

Many reasons, however, inclined them to preserve their allegiance to the Byzantine court, or at least to refrain from transferring it to any other potentate. Old associations, and the fear of change, would have their weight in determining the course pursued; but the circumstances which chiefly influenced the Popes in their decision were, in the first place, the distance of Constantinople from Rome, which was favourable to their independence; and, in the next, the declining power and feeble character of the Emperors, which rendered them convenient masters to aspiring vassals.

The evident intention of the Bishops of Rome, to play off the Langobards and the Byzantine court against each other, and to make their own career the resultant of these two opposing forces, seemed, for some time, likely to be entirely frustrated. The iconoclastic controversy, with all its horrible and ridiculous consequences, now began to agitate the Christian world, and gave rise to the bitterest hostility between the great capitals of the East and West, and their respective rulers. The Emperor Leo III., surnamed the Isaurian, disgusted at the idolatrous worship paid by his subjects to the images which filled the churches, issued, in *A. D.* 726, his famous decree for their destruction.

It was then that the independence of thought and action to which the Roman bishops had accustomed themselves was clearly manifested. The emperor communicated his pleasure respecting the destruction of the images to the Pope, and claimed from him the same unanswering obedience which he was accustomed to meet with from the Patriarch of Constantinople. But Gregory II., encouraged by the unanimous support of the Italians, who looked to him as the champion of their beloved idols, not only refused, in a letter full of personal abuse, to carry out the wishes of the emperor, but fulminated a threat of excommunication against all who should dare to lay violent hands upon the images.

After so public a renunciation of his allegiance, we might expect to see the Bishop of Rome avowedly siding with the Langobards, especially as they had forsaken the Arian heresy, and their King Luitprand himself had manifested a very high degree of veneration for St. Peter's chair. But the motives suggested above retained their force, and no such change took place; on the contrary, we are told that when the Italians, "on hearing the wickedness of Leo, formed a plan of electing a new emperor and conducting him to Constantinople," the Pope induced them to forego their purpose and adhere to their former allegiance.

★★★★★★

Epist. Gregor. ii. ad Leon. The two letters addressed by Gregory II. to the emperor were written after 730 A. D. Vid. Gieseler's Kirchengesch. ii. Among other things he tells the emperor: "Even the little children mock thee! Wander through the elementary schools, and say 'I am the destroyer and the persecutor of the images,' and they will immediately throw their slates at thy head! . . . Thou hast written, 'Hosiah, King of the Jews (the holy Father means Hezekiah: 2 Kings, xviii. 4.), after 800 years, brought the brazen serpent out of the Temple; and I, after 800 years, have brought the images out of the Churches.' Truly Hosiah was thy brother, and had the same faith, and tyrannised over the priests of that time as thou dost now." (2 Chron. xxvi. 16-18.). The ultramontane writers have cited this as an example in which an heretical emperor was deprived of a part of his dominions by the fiat of the Papal Chair.

★★★★★★

Nor is his policy on this occasion difficult to understand. The Langobards were too near, and the absorption of Rome into their empire would have been too complete to allow the Bishops of Rome free scope for their lofty schemes of ambition. As subjects of King Luitprand, they would have run the risk of sinking from the rank of virtual rulers of the Roman duchy, to that of mere metropolitan bishops. And the danger of this degradation grew every day more urgent. Gregory II. died in the midst of the perplexities arising from his critical position. But the same policy was pursued by his successor Gregory III. with so much determination, that Luitprand, who—whatever may have been his reverence for the spiritual character of his opponent, and liberal as he was towards the Holy See—could not overlook his intrigues, and was determined to be sole master in Italy, found it necessary to advance upon Rome with a hostile army.

The scruples which the pious Langobard may have felt in violating St. Peter's patrimony, must have been greatly relieved by the very secular conduct of Gregory in respect to the king's rebellious vassals. Thrasamund, Duke of Spoleto, having incurred the displeasure of his sovereign, took refuge in Rome; and when Luitprand demanded that he should be given up, the Pope and the Patricians of the Romans united in giving a decided refusal. (Paull. Diac.) The opposition to Luitprand was further strengthened by the adhesion of Gottschalk, Duke of Benevento, who took up arms against his suzerain; and in an engagement which took place soon after, between the king and his mutinous vassals, Roman troops were seen fighting on the side of the rebels.

Contrary to the hopes and expectations of Gregory, Luitprand was completely victorious; and, justly irritated by the conduct of the Romans, to whom he had shown so much forbearance, immediately led his forces to the very gates of Rome, with the full intention of incorporating it with the rest of his Italian dominions; and thus, with all his foresight, Gregory had brought the rising structure of the papacy into the greatest danger, and appeared to be himself at the mercy of his enemies.

In this extremity the holy father bethought himself of the powerful and orthodox nation which had for so many ages been the faithful ally of the Catholic Church, and had lately been united in still closer bonds of reverence and amity to St. Peter's chair. In *A.D.* 739, Pope Gregory III. applied for aid against the Langobards "to his most excellent son, the Sub-King Carl." (Fredeg. *Chron. Cont.*)

That this application was made unwillingly, and with considerable misgivings about the consequences, may be inferred from the extremities to which Gregory submitted before he made it.

His hesitation was owing, no doubt, in part to his instinctive dread of giving the papal chair a too powerful protector, who might easily become a master; and partly to his knowledge of the sincere friendship which existed between his opponent Luitprand and his desired ally. Of all the circumstances which threatened to prevent the realisation of the papal dreams of temporal independence and spiritual domination, none were so greatly and so justly dreaded as an alliance between the Franks and Langobards; and we shall see that Gregory III. and his successors spared no pains, and shrunk from no means however questionable, to excite jealousy and hatred between the Franks and their Lombard kinsmen.

While the Romans were trembling within their hastily-repaired walls, and awaiting the decisive assault of the Langobards, Carl Martel was resting from the fatigues of his late campaigns in Burgundy; and he was still in that country when the papal envoys reached him. They brought with them a piteous epistle from Gregory, in which he complains with bitterness of the persecutions of his enemies, who, he says, had robbed the very church of St. Peter (which stood without the walls) of its candlesticks; and taken away the pious offerings of the Frankish princes. (*Cod. Carol.*) Carl received the communication of the afflicted Pontiff with the greatest reverence. The interests of the empire, and more especially of his own family, were too intimately connected with the existence and honour of the Bishops of Rome, to allow of his feeling indifferent to what was passing in Italy; and there is no reason to doubt that he entertained the highest veneration for the Head of the Church. Yet this first embassy seems to have justified the fears rather than the hopes of Gregory.

The incessant exertions which Carl's enemies compelled him to make for the maintenance of his authority would long ago have destroyed a man of ordinary energy and endurance, and were beginning to tell even upon his iron frame. He was aware that the new order of things, of which he was the principal author, depended for its continuance and consolidation solely upon his presence and watchfulness. So far from being in a condition to lead his forces to a distant country, and to make enemies of brave and powerful friends, it was not long since he had sought the assistance of the Langobards themselves; and he knew not how soon he might stand in need of it again. He therefore contented himself with opening friendly negotiations with Luitprand, who excused himself to Carl, and agreed to spare the Papal territory on condition that the Romans should cease to interfere between himself and his rebellious subjects.

The exact terms of the agreement made between Gregory and Luitprand, by the mediation of Carl Martel, are of the less moment, as they were observed by neither party. In *A. D.* 740 the Langobards again appeared in arms before the gates of Rome; and the Pope was once more a suppliant at the Frankish court. In the letter which Carl Martel received on this occasion, Gregory bitterly complains that no effectual aid had been as yet afforded him; that more attention had been paid to the "lying" reports of the Lombard king than to his own statements, and he earnestly implores his "most Christian son" not to prefer the friendship of Luitprand to the love of the Prince of the Apostles.

★★★★★★

Cod. Carol. Epist. i., ii. It seems but fair to the memory of Luitprand to quote the words of the historian of the Langobards respecting him. "(Luitprand) was a man of great wisdom, wise in council, God-fearing, and a friend of peace. He was powerful in battle, merciful towards sinners, chaste and temperate, watchful in prayer, generous to the poor, unacquainted indeed with the sciences, but worthy of being considered equal to the philosophers, a father of his people and a reformer of the laws.

—Paull. Diacon. *Hist. Langob. lib.* vi.

★★★★★★

It is evident from the whole tenor of this second epistle, that the Frankish mayor had not altered his conduct towards the King of the Lombards, in consequence of Gregory's charges and complaints; but had trusted rather to his own knowledge of his friend than to the invectives of the terrified and angry Pope.

To give additional weight to his written remonstrances and entreaties, Gregory sent the bishop, Anastasius, and the presbyter, Sergius, to Carl Martel, charged with more secret and important instructions, which he scrupled to commit to writing. The nature of their communications may be gathered from the symbolical actions by which they were accompanied. The envoys brought with them the keys of St. Peter's sepulchre, which they offered to Carl, on whom they were also empowered to confer the title and dignity of Roman *Patricius*. (Fredeg. *Chron. Cont.*; *Annal. Mett.* an. 741 also mention St. Peter's chains among the offerings.) By the former step—the offer of the keys (an honour never before conferred upon a Frankish ruler)—Gregory expressed his desire to constitute the powerful mayor Protector of the Holy See; and by conferring the rank of Roman *Patricius* without, as seems probable, the sanction of the Greek Emperor, he in effect withdrew his allegiance from the latter, and acknowledged Carl Martel as liege lord of the Roman duchy and people.

It was in this light that the whole transaction was regarded at the time, for we read in the chronicle of Moissiac, written in the beginning of the ninth century, that the letter of the Pope was accompanied by "a decree of the Roman *Principes*;" and that the Roman people, having thrown off the rule of the Greek Emperor, desired to place themselves under the protection of the "aforesaid prince, and his invincible clemency."

Carl Martel received the ambassadors with the distinguished honour due to the dignity of the sender, and the importance of their mission; and willingly accepted at their hands the significant offerings they brought. When they were prepared to return, he loaded them with costly presents, and ordered Grimo, the Abbot of Corbey, and Sigebert, a monk of St. Denis, to accompany them to Rome, and bear his answer to Pope Gregory. Rome was once more delivered from destruction by the intervention of Carl, and his influence with Luitprand.

And thus, were the last days of the great Frankish hero and Gregory III. employed in marking out a line of policy respecting each other, and the great temporal and spiritual interests committed to them, which, being zealously followed up by their successors, led in the sequel to the most important and brilliant results. They both died nearly at the same time, in the same year (*A.D.* 741) in which the events above described took place. The restless activity of Carl Martel had prematurely worn him out. Conscious of the rapid decline of his powers, he began to set his house in order; and he had scarcely time to portion out his vast empire among his sons, and to make his peace with heaven in the church of the patron saint, when he was seized by a fever in his palace at Chiersy, on the Oise; where he died on the 15th (or 21st) of October, *A.D.* 741, at the early age of fifty. He was buried in the church of St. Denis.

Carl Martel may be reckoned in the number of those great men who have been deprived of more than half the glory due to them, "because they want the sacred poet." Deeds which, in the full light of history, would have appeared sufficient to make a dozen warriors immortal, are despatched by the Frankish chroniclers in a few dry words. His greatness, indeed, shines forth even from their meagre notices; but we feel, as we read them, that had a Caesar or a Livy unfolded his character and described his exploits,—instead of a poor pedantic monk like Fredegar,—a rival might be found for the Caesars, the Scipios, and the Hannibals.

We have seen that he inherited little from his father but the hereditary vigour of his race. He began life as the prisoner of an envious stepmother. When he escaped from his prison at Cologne, he was surrounded by powerful enemies; nor could he consider himself safe until, with a force which voluntarily joined his standard, he had defeated three armies larger than his own. His subsequent career was in accordance with the deeds of his early life.

Every step in his onward progress was the result of a contest. He fought his way to the seat of his mighty father. He defeated the Neustrians, and compelled them to receive a sovereign at his hands. He attacked and defeated, in rapid succession, the warlike nations of the Frisians and the Saxons; he refixed the Frankish yoke more firmly upon the necks of the Swabians, the Bavarians, the Aquitanians, and Gascons; and, above all, he stemmed the mighty tide of Moslemism which threatened to engulf the then known world.

Nor was it with external enemies alone that he had to contend. To the last days of his active life he was engaged in quelling the endless seditions of the great *seigniors*, who were as impatient of control from above as of opposition from below.

His mighty deeds are recorded; but of the manner in which he set about them; of the resources, internal and external, mental and physical, by which he was enabled to perforin them; of his personal character and habits; of his usual dwelling-place; of his friends and servants, his occupations, tastes, and habits, we are left in the profoundest ignorance.

The great and important results of his activity were the predominance of the German element in the Frankish empire, the preservation of Europe from Mohammedanism, and the union of the principal German tribes into one powerful State. And all these mighty objects he effected, as far as we are able to judge, chiefly, though not entirely, by the sword. He beat down everything which barred his course; he crushed all those who dared to oppose him; he coerced the stubbornness of the independent German tribes, and welded them together by terrific and repeated blows. Our prevailing idea of him, therefore, is that of force—irresistible energy; and his popular surname of Martel, or the Hammer, appears a particularly happy one.

The task which he performed was in many respects similar to that of Clovis at an earlier period; but it is not difficult to see that it was performed in a very different spirit. Guizot says (*Essais*):

He is not an ordinary usurper. He is the chief of a new people which has not renounced its ancient manners, and which holds more closely to Germany than to Gaul.

Though superior to Clovis, even as a warrior, we have no sufficient reason to accuse Carl Martel of being either treacherous or cruel. The incessant wars in which he was unavoidably engaged, necessarily imply a great amount of confusion in the State, and of sacrifice and suffering on the part of the people. And we have sufficient evidence of a direct nature, to show that the usual effects of long-continued wars were severely felt in the Frankish empire. The great mass of the people is seldom honoured by the notice of the Chroniclers, and never except in their relation to those for whom they toil and bleed; and we might have been left in blissful ignorance of the cost of Carl Martel's brilliant deeds, had not the coffers of the Church been heavily mulcted to defray it.

Ecclesiastical property, which, at the time we speak of, comprised a large proportion of the land, was exempted, by various immunities and privileges, from bearing its due share of the public burdens. Carl Martel, therefore, to whom a large and constant supply of money was indispensable, was accustomed to make a portion of the wealth of the Church available to the wants of the State. This he effected by bestowing bishoprics and rich benefices on his personal friends and trustiest followers, without much regard to their fitness for the clerical office. It was for this offence that, notwithstanding the support he gave to Boniface and his brother missionaries, and the number of churches which he founded and endowed, he was held up by ecclesiastical writers of a later age as a destroyer of monasteries, "who converted the property of the Church to his own use," and on that account died "a fearful death."

★★★★★★

This passage (which is without doubt an interpolation) is found in the *Epistola Bonifacii, 72 ad Ethelbaldum Regem*, in which Ethelbald is reminded of the melancholy fate of the Kings Ceolred and Osred, who died an early death for having destroyed monasteries. William of Malmesbury has adopted the interpolation of which neither of the above-mentioned editors could find a trace in the most ancient

MSS.Vid. Roth, Beneficialwesen.

★★★★★★

More than a hundred years after Carl's decease (in *A. D.* 858) Louis, the German, was reminded, by a synod held at Chiersy, of the sins committed by his great ancestor against the Church. The assembled fathers said to the king:

> Prince Carl, the father of Pepin, who was the first among the Frankish kings and princes to alienate and distribute the goods of the Church, was solely on that account eternally damned.

They then proceeded to relate the well-known *Visio S. Eucherii*, a forgery of Archbishop Hinemar, according to which, Eucherius, Bishop of Orleans, having been transported to the other world in a trance, beheld Carl Martel suffering the pains of hell. On his inquiring, of the angel who accompanied him, the reason of what he saw, he was told that the mighty *major-domus* was suffering the penalty of having seized and distributed the property of the Church. The astonished bishop related what had befallen him to Boniface, and Fulrad the abbot of St. Denis, and repaired in their company to the sepulchre of Carl Martel. On opening the coffin, which was charred on the inside and contained no corpse, a dragon rushed out and made its escape. (*Vita Eucherii.* Unfortunately for the credibility of the romantic story, the *Vit. Euchar.* shows that the dreaming prelate died three years before Carl Martel, as is proved by Roth (*Beneficialwesen.*)

Against these and other harsh judgments of the great hero's character (none of which are earlier than the ninth century), the acrimonious nature of which betrays their source, we may set the respect of his contemporaries, the friendship of Boniface and Pope Gregory, and the fact that he endowed and enriched a great number of religious houses, and was frequently applied to by the Pope to defend St. Peter's chair. That his own necessities, and the excessive wealth and troublesome privileges of the Church, induced him to take measures which operated injuriously on the character of the clergy, cannot be denied; but he proved in many ways that he acted in no hostile spirit to religion or its ministers, but under the pressure of circumstances which he could not control. If he used a portion of the revenues of the Church to pay and equip his soldiers, he led those soldiers against the bitterest enemies of Christendom, the heathen and the Moslem. His lot was cast in the battlefield, but the part which he there performed was useful as well as brilliant.

Though evidently a warrior of the highest class—great in the council as in the field—he was not that degraded being, a mere warrior. He never seems to have sought war for its own sake, or to have delighted in bloodshed. He was willing to negotiate with an enemy, even when he felt himself the stronger; and was placable and generous to his bitterest foes. The aid he afforded to Boniface and others in their efforts to convert the heathen, and the sympathy he showed in their success, sufficiently prove that he was not indifferent to religion; and that he could appreciate, not only the brave exploits of the gallant soldier, but the self-sacrificing labours of the zealous missionary.